PINTEREST MARKETING AMPLIFICATION

7 METHODS TO AMPLIFY YOUR REACH AND BOOST SALES CONVERSIONS

KERRIE LEGEND

KERRIE LEGEND
WRITER & DESIGNER

PRAISE FOR KERRIE LEGEND

Kerrie knows her stuff. If this is going to be like her other books, this will be filled with hands-on information you can use to grow your audience with Pinterest. ~ *Review of Pinterest Marketing.*

TRICIA LYNNE

If you are looking to up your marketing game, this is the book for you. Kerrie is practically handing you success. Read this book now if you want to be able to compete in your area of business. ~ *Review of Pinterest Marketing.*

T. CRANE

Kerrie does it again with another remarkably comprehensive Pinterest book designed for people who have read Pinterest Marketing already. It's filled with all sorts of meaty details that help you make the connection between leveraging the power of pinning using 7 methods created and documented by the author and specific marketing tasks that impact other marketing must-haves like SEO and organic search.

PIPER HOUGHES, BOOK REVIEWER AT
PIPERBOOKBLOG.COM

To my family, a bunch of Pinterest nerds.

Joe - trucker toys

Logan (age 10) - step by step drawing doodles

Kade (age 8) - slime

Colt (age 7) - Minecraft printables

Joey (age 4) - charcuterie boards

Koda (age 3) - Legos

Jackson (age 3) - dinosaurs

Kerrie - hygge lifestyle

I love you, you awesome nerds.

FOREWORD

Have you ever researched something with such intense interest that you became an expert about it? Or was there a time where you made a discovery or had a major ah-ha moment that changed part of your life forever? Or a time in your life where a single moment of success triggered insatiable joy?

The Story

Remembering the day I published Pinterest Marketing: 80k to 14+ Million in 3 Months brings a lot of smiles in my house. *Mommy's Pinterest book.* There was a sense of accomplishment, relief, and giddy excitement because I was finally able to share publicly everything I did to grow my Pinterest presence in three months. To say I was excited to share that book with the world would be an understatement.

I wanted to tell the whole world about just how powerful Pinterest Marketing can be.

There was a lot of testing and research done in the months between December 2018 and February 2019 in our house over a kitchen table. It was intense. Initially my husband, Joe, didn't understand my obsession. But then, after a few days of consistent growth and documenting numbers in my bullet journal, he was hooked into this intense focus of documenting results.

"What's your number today?"

My husband and I looked forward to 4 p.m. every day, which was when the new analytics were posted.

"I don't know yet... they haven't posted the updates to analytics yet."

What would the results be? We waited with eager anticipation, usually with a charcuterie board in front of us with a glass of wine as we wrapped up the day's schoolwork with the boys, stumbling on Legos as we shared new ideas we found on Pinterest with each other. The glow of the iPhone screens shone brightly on our faces while we pinned away and stashed new ideas we found for later.

I'll admit it. We're a family of Pinterest nerds.

The dark days of winter were filled with hard work in creating, posting, pinning, researching, evaluating analytics, running numbers... watching. Observing. Listening to what the numbers meant. Interpreting. Confusion, success, frustration, elated emotions.

Create more content. Test it. Write more. Get some new images together. Pin, pin, pin. I was obsessed. Excited. It was working.

Post-Christmas, I started creating even more pillar content, playing around with content pieces, pin designs, working on efficient methods of pinning and marketing, documenting image releases, researching tribes, calculating reach impact to re-shares and re-pin statistics, recording results, and writing. Lots of writing. Outlining, mostly, but yeah. Writing.

Finally, February 28 rolled around. It was the end of our research and testing timeframe.

"14 million today."

He gave me an incredulous stare. The Pinterest analytics had rolled over from 13.9 million monthly views to 14 overnight.

"Holy crap. And sales? Page views?"

I smiled. You know... that kind of smile the flashes across your face after a long project comes to a successful completion.

"450k page views on my blog. Sales are the highest they've ever been. I officially don't have to do design services anymore if I don't want to."

It was a day we had looked forward to for years. I could stop designing for people or be more choosy about who to do design work for, increase my rates, and focus on writing and my own projects.

"When you say 'Yes' to others, make sure you are not saying 'No' to yourself."

PAOLO COEHLO

Time is a resource we treasure as we mold and create a lifestyle centered around family, self-employment, small business, and homeschooling. My time had become so consumed with doing work for others over the years I had been telling myself "no" for a lot of things I wanted to create and do. We finally got out of the service trap.

When you're a Pinterest nerd, willing and ready to try and discover new things, that's a hard thing to swallow. *I can't. I don't have time.*

Before the winter of 2018/2019, we had mediocre success with Pinterest. Average success for any blogger, really, with the numbers I was posting. But we had *finally* cracked the case on Pinterest by the end of February 2019. We succeeded in our own time, our own way. I had to share everything I knew about it in a book and teach all this discovery. I got to writing.

The Book

April came and went, as with the following month's book release for Pinterest Marketing. A chapter was written in it that talked about what I focused on during those months to grow my blog traffic from a meager 75k page views per month to over 450k by the end of February, all thanks to the help of a few Pinterest strategies I used.

And readers loved it. I got so many messages telling me about successes, accomplishments, newly elevated stats, and so on. Everything I shared and recommended to my readers was working for them.

But I still had so much to say and tell you about with Pinterest. I wasn't done.

Don't get me wrong—Pinterest Marketing is a fantastic book. It's great for beginners new to Pinterest marketing and bloggers looking to grow. But looking at it now, with this very book about amplification under my belt, that first book on Pinterest Marketing is only the beginning. So if you're ready to go deeper and pursue blogging as a full-time career, this is your next step.

During those three months of intense Pinterest focus, I had deployed a series of strategies involving content production that at the time of publication, but just hadn't quite put it all down on paper. I knew what I did, but documenting it and formulating words to explain it all was going to take quite some time. An entire summer, actually. And that's how I spent my summer in 2019 besides spending time with my kids.

Because of the title, I wanted to leave the Pinterest Marketing book the way it was. Marketing is one thing. Amplification and methodologies of releasing content to amplify your reach is a whole other animal. Amplification methods should only be used when a Pinterest user has a firm understanding of how Pinterest works, how to set everything up, pin design, analytics, etc. Amplification methods will take you even further into the world of professional blogging. So if you haven't read Pinterest Marketing: 80k to 14+ Million in 3 Months yet, now is a good time to pick that one up and read that first.

The Sequel... to Continue Learning About Pinterest

After documenting it all, I came to realize I had established 7 different methods of amplification. Once I realized I had established "methods", I had to go back and rewrite a few thing to put it all in context. These seven methods that will help you create better, long-lasting content that garners much more traffic that what you might already be doing. Methods that will help you focus more on remarkable content and search.

Pinterest Marketing Amplification was finally born in September 2019. All the content and pinning methods I used to grow to over 14+ million monthly viewers (and stay above 10 million with consistent blog traffic over 400k page views a month), along with screenshots, examples of content, and how-to information finally came together.

Let me tell you—putting a book together about something you created or formed into a method is a lot of hard work. But I'm glad I did it, and I think you'll be glad I slung some ink on paper.

So here's your invitation to learn something brand new. A topic that has never been discussed by anyone, and one you won't find on any blogs... *because it was created by me.*

Do not try to do everything. Do one thing well.

STEVE JOBS

This is the one thing I'm really good at, and I'm glad I wrote this book so you can learn, too. I'm relieved it's finished. *Excited for you.* There's a LOT of insight I've learned and wanted to document for you in here. So I hope you learn a lot and become a better writer and more efficient marketer as a result.

I look at blogging as my job. This is my career choice, and I love it. Focusing on and mastering Pinterest has made my blogging job joyful. Easy. I find myself less concerned about what other people think, and am on a mission to make relationships with the audience I tend to attract who are sitting in front of Netflix on a Saturday night working on their home-based business, devouring a pint of ice cream and snuggling with their dog. The kind of people who need help in how to blog. And, I'm more focused with challenging myself and designing products.

"Everything that's good that's happened to me in my life came because of that. I may not do everything great in my life…I'm not perfect… but I'm good at this, and I want to share this with you. I want to teach you what I learned. I get to touch peoples' lives with what I do. And it keeps me going and I love it. And I think if you give it a shot you might love it, too. "

CARL CASPER, "CHEF" BY JON
FAVREAU

I want you to experience the joy of having such an intense interest about something that you grow both personally and professionally from it. I want you to learn, to absorb, and to experience all of those ah-ha moments I once had. I'd love for you to succeed, too.

Now, let's talk amplification and get to it.

Happy reading and creating, my friend.

INTRODUCTION

Why amplify on Pinterest? Isn't pinning 4 images per post or page enough? Shouldn't looping pins keep my content in front of Pinterest users? Is paying for tribes in Tailwind really worth it? Why should I worry about spreading out my images and evaluate my pinning frequency? What's the deal with promoting ads? Do I need to spend money in order to be found? How can I get more people to be more aware of my brand? None of my landing pages are converting even though I get a lot of Pinterest traffic—what am I doing wrong?

So many questions. I have a lot of answers for you.

Pinterest Marketing Amplification focuses intensely on content creation, efficient pinning, and search, so you can get back to writing and creating. For example, how to get more pins out there streaming in a steady flow of pre-qualified readers to your website. Numbers and analytics—what matters and what to look at closer than what you might currently be. The mindset of the user. Writing clever headlines, making preview pins and drawing a pre-qualified audience into your world.

But most importantly, how to get you to the point where you have a winning strategy—defined as incoming sales so routine that you're able to rank on whatever platform you're selling on, be able to count on a more frequent sales trend, and plan new products with confidence.

Create remarkable posts so you can use pieces of it to build your pillars of content. Spend more time creating and writing while Pinterest helps you find your future customers who are already expressing an interest in what you offer.

That's why we're on Pinterest in the first place, right? To find our people. To get them to see us for the talented writers and creators and sources of inspiration that we are. To generate sales.

I have looked forward to writing this book for so long. Took three months to document and get everything down in an organized fashion for you, but it was worth it. YOU, my reader, are worth it.

Let's climb to the top of Pinterest so you can see all of the domain traffic you've been missing out on.

I fricking love this book. I hope you will, too.

PINTEREST MARKETING AMPLIFICATION

1 CONTENT MODIFIER METHOD

TO AMPLIFY YOUR REACH, you need content. You need to be writing and creating content regularly to get things moving. After you grow, you can slow down and create over time. But initially, as part of the amplification process, you're going to create some critical foundation content, also known as pillar content, to start getting a steady flow of traffic in to your website.

You can't amplify with 5 short blog posts and a 5-page website. It just won't work that way. I tested that out, and the results failed miserably. Creating valuable content and plenty of it, starting out in this journey to amplify and grow your Pinterest account will not only benefit your growth, but your readers will appreciate the effort, too. That appreciation will come to light in the form of sales.

The first method I want to introduce you to is the content

modifier method. This method is largely based off of the concept of creating pillar content or long-form blog posts (macro content), and then making micro content from it in different forms of posts or content pieces, including spin-offs into deeper content for other macro content. In effect, you're amplifying your reach both organically for SEO and also on Pinterest.

The goal is to establish the ability to create an abundance of Pinterest pins for more visibility and increase the probability of click-through conversion, while avoiding getting the account labeled for spam.

Long-form, pillar content and Pinterest complement each other beautifully, and this is a method you can use to build loyal readers and fans of your work while modifying your content to test, create more content with less effort, and fill your editorial calendar. This is a method I researched while building my Pinterest account and I found that my pillar content sustained greater, longer attention than all of my shorter blog posts combined. But it also allowed me to take my subheader content and go more in-depth and create another micro piece of content around it.

Let's break down what goes into creating pillar content and how you can implement this into your Pinterest game plan. First, a quick study on long-form blog posts so you understand the premise of how this method is superior to what you might already be doing.

Long-Form Blog Posts

Long-form blog content allows you to provide more value in a single post. The point of a long-form post isn't to reach a particular word count for the sake of that word count, but instead to provide so much valuable information that it reaches or exceeds a particular word count.

Some experts will say that long-form blog posts are a huge gamble. There's just too much information for a reader's limited timespan of attention. That attention span seems to shorten 10 seconds every single day. But why?

I have a theory. There's too much crap content out there for a reader to feel like they should invest their time in rending a blog post. Keyboard warrior experts with only a little real, worthy experience worth noting are everywhere. Some are writing just for the money, others writing to get to a word count, and others, well, just don't know how to write posts that matter enough for an audience to care.

Other experts say that writing longer posts and articles engages readers on a more personal and professional level, offering them a more rewarding and genuine experience.

So who is right?

The long-form experts have been proven right time and time again, statistically speaking. In evaluating all the research and tests done between Neil Patel, Jeff Goins, and other incredible writers, I have not seen short blogs win this content race. Ever. Ultimately, you should create long-form content because it will get you more of what you want: more online visibility (social shares, links), proof of your authority and industry expertise, and envy-inducing material for magnanimous community building and engagement.

Specifically, here are a few things you'll get from one piece of long-form content:

SEO Gone Wrong - Why Short is Going to Hurt You

When blogging first became "a thing", SEO experts were screaming at us left and right about how you need to use keywords and blog often even if it was something short. As long as something new was given to Google to appease the robot with the right words, you were "blogging". The realm of SEO keyword stuffing emerged, and content was just a spattered mess with nothing really coherent or valuable attached to it. Long-term relationships were not developed. Blogs were reduced to meaningless statistics and not valued for the relationship between the blogger and the reader.

Bloggers were told by "experts" to create blog post after blog post—daily even—to grow in rank and appease the gods of Google. And as a result, the scammy, slimy marketer of the online environment was born. "Systems" were being sold that did nothing but force the reader into buying into other products and coaching plans they couldn't afford just to "make it" online.

That was, until the long-form blog post and emergence of Pinterest came around back in early 2012. Now, don't get me wrong. Occasionally you'll find the lingering ClickBank-type sales page with yellow and red lettering floating around the web. A whole new world opened up where readers could actually learn something new without having to fork over money for it. *A beautiful thing.* To be entertained, inspired, and educated all in one. *The blogging world is one of many teachers and experiences.* Thanks to Pinterest, we've evolved as a blogging community in that we're able to educate our readers, inspire them to improve their lives, and entertain them at the same time.

Now, the online world is filled with short blog posts. As short as 300 words, which is not a lot of content at all. 300 words covers three paragraphs. Can you really develop a trusting, long-term relationship with your readers over 300 words on a blog post?

This reminds me of a Walmart scenario and the kind of people that can't seem to return their cart to the cart corral. They spent all this time gathering groceries and going through checkout, but to ask them to return the cart to the designated area to prevent vehicle or bodily damage is just too much.

They just couldn't see the process through or give enough of themselves, out of respect for others, to see the process through to the end.

The cart whizzes across the parking lot with a comical speed and crashes into an unsuspecting Honda Civic. Inner rage ensues and the owner of said vehicle waves a clenched fist in the air. How dare you, sir! Don't worry, I'm getting to a point.

How many times have you read a blog post that only skimmed the surface and offered nothing more? How many blog posts have you stumbled on that were filled with vague advice? Or left you wondering... *is that all you got on this topic? Surely there's more to this...*

Those are not feelings readers experience that build trust and loyalty with a brand or a blogger. Sadly, I fell under the frame of thought by buying into the whole "push content for SEO" thing. I thought pushing out endless blog posts that popped into my head when I first started out was the answer. Ha! Nope. I look at some of my earlier stuff and while I was on a good path, my writing sucked. I wanted the readers. But I wasn't earning them.

You'll learn valuable, and sometimes, costly lessons as you grow as a blogger and writer. Short blogs and short content, while appealing to the eyes of the reader, will ultimately hurt you, and them, in the end. There are better ways to capture attention (like using headers, subheaders, images, quotes, graphics, etc.) and give your reader exactly what they're hoping to get from you.

This is Pinterest, after all. Your reader is a savvy user who is also a natural shopper. A purveyor of everything new that brings joy to life. Who craves to learn and try new things.

And if there's one thing that I've learned from Gary Vaynerchuk, who is a constant source of insight into this crazy world of social media, search, and marketing, it's that you have to cater to the mindset of the platform that the user is on. Here's what I know for sure:

- *You don't put 300-word blog posts on your site. That could be done in a Facebook or LinkedIn post.*
- *You have to remember what the platform you're marketing on and why the user enjoys coming to that platform.*
- *serpIQ did a research study and noted that articles and posts over 2000 in word length scored in the top 10 ranks for search inquiries.*
- *Long-form blog posts will give you more micro content to work with and spin off from.*

Short form blog posts have no place in your Pinterest game plan. If you've been blogging 300-1000 word pieces, stop. Creating more and more short-form articles for the purpose of getting more opportunities for keyword stuffing out there is not a solid strategy. What IS a solid strategy is creating content off of existing content to support the macro content or pillar content you write, and have more pinning opportunities from your site.

Little articles only send the message to a reader that you don't care enough to see the topic all the way through. If this means that you write less blog posts altogether, then so be it. But if you're consistently blogging articles below 2000 words, know that you can probably add some stories, relatable experience, and share some more research than what you've already written to lengthen it out and give value.

And creating more value is something I talked about in Email Marketing Magic quite a bit. Your readers crave something more than a quick, vague snippet about something you're an expert about and then be pushed into a product in order to the get answer. *There is value in your wisdom.* Why not create blog posts that actually solve a problem or a challenge? Or share insight? Or share your discoveries? That would be amazing. Never be afraid to share your ideas and thoughts in the mindset that you won't make sales or that you're giving too much away. The reverse is going to happen.

There is something authoritative about long-form content. Would you trust a 500-word post about Pinterest or a 50,000-word book about Pinterest and all the specific intricacies? Not only do search engines love it, but a study of Wikipedia articles indicated that increasing the length of a blog post or article increased its trustworthiness.

Try writing longer articles. Not the navel-gazing type stuff of course, or long diatribes about something you're not passionate about, but instead, sharing discoveries, new things you've created to solve a problem you had, or even insight you've gleamed from an experience is all helpful, provided it's in-depth and conquers a problem or challenge. You'd be so amazing and valued as a writer if you switched it up into something much more value-driven.

When I started writing 1000+ word articles instead of shorter ones, I started noticing a difference. I was getting a lot more traffic naturally, even without Pinterest. But the return traffic wasn't quite there yet. A brand search was revealing an organic post I was known for regarding Scrivener for bloggers, but nothing else, really, at the time. Bounce rate and page abandons went down, and time on site as well as user engagement went up.

But when I started generating 2000-word blog posts (the new standard of long-form writing) I noticed a huge difference. Time on site was way up. Additional page reads were up. The new average was 5 pages per visit. Bounce rate went WAY down, and my overall page views per session increased. Finally, returning sessions went up, as well. There was a time on my site when 90% of my traffic was all new. That largely explains the email list I developed, but I'd much rather have devoted fans and loyal readers than new ones all the time.

So I stuck with it. I saved a lot of my greatest writing for my email marketing, and generated long-form articles on pages instead of within my blog, just to test things out on Pinterest. It worked beautifully. And now that the testing has confirmed something I had suspected all along… that writing long-form articles, even though it took much more time and effort, were the way to go. And with my Pinterest strategies in the other hand, there was a way to make long-form content partner with a fantastic pinning strategy. Voila.

What you'll find is that as user engagement and length of time on your site increases, your email list also increases at the same time.

Bottom line—long form content doesn't just resonate with search engines and Pinterest users—it resonates with your audience, creating trust and loyalty. Long form is so much better than short form, and now you're going to find out how it relates to Pinterest and creating content from that macro pillar content. Plus, long-form content is evergreen (which Pinterest users love), so it'll continue to gain traffic for years to come, not just within weeks after you publish it.

Getting Started with the Content Modifier Method

Alright so let's break this down into steps and make this easy now that you have the argument in favor of long-form posts and meatier articles. This is going to play into the other methods of amplification beautifully, so it's not a method to miss.

The first thing you need to do is write something related to a topic in your niche that you're intensely interested in. Approach this with joy. *Be excited.* You're about to solve a LOT of challenges for some people craving your kind of expertise and insight. Let's do this.

Remarkable content takes time to create. But I know you're going to do a fantastic job once you know what to do with Pinterest as your primary plan.

So because we're doing long-form writing with Pinterest in mind, we're going to write blog posts or pages directly on your website. Nowhere else (initially). Your website is where you keep all of your long-form content. Let's go back to blogging long-form 101 so that you can make sure you have the right information and no assumptions getting in your way.

Pillar Content Long-Form 101

Go back to blogging 101. Start with laying out your plan for your content. Write with a plan in mind.

What's the strategy?

- For backlinks, focus on in-depth "how-to", listicles and "why" style content pieces.
- For a high rate of shares, focus on visual content, especially infographics and pretty pin pictures.
- For getting new leads to add to your email marketing sales funnel (see Email Marketing Magic for this), focus on gated content such as workbooks, guides, case studies, whitepapers, product brochures and webinars.

Begin your blog post plan by thinking about these things:

- Keywords and search queries (What are people looking for?)
- Existing analytics (What content do you already have, maybe on your blog, that's performing well?)
- Target audience (Who are you going after? What makes them tick? What do you know about them?)
- Competition (What else is out there? Can you beat it?)

- Email sign-up buttons (Make it easy for people to get more of your content.)
- Links to other content (If this particular piece of long-form content doesn't fit the reader, you might have something else that works better. Make that easy to find.)
- The next step (Make signing up for a newsletter, reading another piece of content, or sharing the piece on social obvious and easy.)
- Buttons to share on Twitter, Facebook, LinkedIn, etc. (On every page, make it super easy to share the content.)

THE OUTLINE PROCESS

Start outlining your content. The outline is an important piece of the content modifier method, because you're going to use your outline points to develop pin headlines and provoking, intriguing questions. These will also be great for later, when you create landing pages. Start off by creating a broad outline of your content's core sections. Then, you can dive deeper into specifics of each subheader item.

You're following a specific tier system. A parent topic, with child subheaders that will allow you create other micro content. After this parent/child tree you've created for your outline, you can choose to expand each point further, or you can dive in and start writing your content.

No matter how good your content is, only 20% of your content will actually be read on average.

Appeal to the skimmers of your audience! Keep your content concise, scannable, and skimmer-friendly to ensure readers get all the important information without having to read the entire thing if they choose not to. (There are some readers that will read every. single. word.)

This means you will want to:

- use short paragraphs
- keep your sentences a bit shorter
- incorporate bullet points when you can
- identify words or phrases you want your reader to remember and put them in **bold** or *italics* or underline

Let me show you how to outline and use subheaders to help you create micro content after you create this macro content piece, or your pillar content.

RECOMMENDED Pillar Content Outline

Heading

[Blog Post Title]

The title of your blog post should be rich with SEO long-tail keywords, about 60 characters or less. It should be a title a person would search for.

Introduction

Hook your reader's attention and convince them to read more of your content. What is it about? What are they going to get?

Whether your approach is to add humor, interesting or surprising facts, or asking a question, find a way to make the first lines of your blog posts as attention-grabbing as possible. What makes you want to keep reading an article? A quick few paragraphs to draw the reader in is all it takes to get the hook. This should be about 100-200 words in total. Make sure you highlight:

- *Why what you're talking about is important*
- *Who the post applies to*
- *What you're covering [10 ways to spread cheer, how to spread cheer for the holidays, cheer-filled events you'll want to take part in this holiday season, etc.]*

Note: This is a suggested outline. Choose the parts from the recommended outline below that you believe will fit well in your pillar content page.

You'll also notice a prompt with each subheader that allows you to include a link to a supporting post. You'll be creating supporting posts and pages *after* you complete your pillar content. You can jot in a draft URL for each one or create the permalink as you go by using an editorial calendar.

Paragraph 1

Subheader 1: What is [insert topic, content, noun] (and Why Does it Matter)?

Give your article some framework, in case your reader, who is coming directly from Pinterest, isn't familiar with the topic you're writing about. If it's a fairly common topic, create a unique spin or something extraordinary to bring a surprise element to your topic.

Explaining the term or concept gives your reader context and you provide more depth with what you're leading up to. You could add personal or business implications, your understanding or experience, or common misconceptions that people often make—even myths—about your topic.

Interested in [topic, content, noun]? Read [Supporting Post]: [include hyperlink for reference]

Paragraph 2

Subheader 2: The History of [insert topic, content, noun]

Here you can delve into the background of your topic. For me, writing about Pinterest, it could be how Pinterest first came about and a lot of the changes it has gone through over the years. How did your topic get to the point it is today? Take them back and share a story.

Interested in more history of [topic, content, noun]? Read [Supporting Post]: [include hyperlink for reference]

Paragraph 3

<u>Subheader 3:</u> Terms to Know About [insert topic, content, noun]

Here you can list out key terms about your topic and meaning of the terms. You can also provide context, clear up any myths, and when/where to use a specific term over the use of another.

Interested in some other important terms to know about [topic, content, noun]? Read [Supporting Post]: [include hyperlink for reference]

Paragraph 4

<u>Subheader 4:</u> The Pros and Cons of [insert topic, content, noun]

Highlight pros, cons, highs and lows, pluses, minuses. Why do you use it or recommend it? What don't you like about the cons? Are there alternatives or workarounds?

Interested in my complete list on pros and cons for [topic, content, noun]? Read [Supporting Post] and get the free download of all the options: [include hyperlink for reference]

Paragraph 5

<u>Subheader 5:</u> # Examples of [insert topic, content, noun]

Give examples of your topic in use or provide images of specific of your topic's examples. Great opportunity for you to come up with your own images and use them as screenshots for your Pinterest posts!

Interested in other examples of [topic, content, noun]? Read [Supporting Post]: [include hyperlink for reference]

Paragraph 6

Subheader 6: How to [Task/Term]

Great opportunity for step-by-step instructions, and also another opportunity to create a separate how-to blog post. You can also draw on benefits of the topic and how to achieve the best result with your topic. Give your readers an outline and some how-to points.

Be clear, concise, and accurate. Give screen shots to assist your user in the process. Also mark the post as one to review every quarter to ensure that your images for your how-to are up to date, as technology changes, and sometimes companies shut down, and the resource you use for a particular topic may not be available anymore.

Important tip—when doing how-to paragraphs, show your work or your process. It's one thing to give bullet points, it's another to show vs. tell. The latter is better. Make it effortless!

Interested in [topic, content, noun]? Read [Supporting Post]: [include hyperlink for reference]

Paragraph 7

Subheader 7: # Tips and Reminders for [insert topic, content, noun]

What's the best way to approach your topic? What tasks are involved to get to success? Help your reader overcome overwhelm and give them the ability to understand your topic better.

Interested in [topic, content, noun]? Read [Supporting Post]: [include hyperlink for reference]

Paragraph 8

Subheader 8: Analyzing [insert topic, content, noun]

Analyze the topic for your audience. Give them insight on how to analyze their own findings and what makes for good or bad results. Help them differentiate between the results.

Interested in learning more about [topic, content, noun] analysis and gauging your results? Read [Supporting Post]: [include hyperlink for reference]

Paragraph 9

Subheader 9: Resources for [insert topic, content, noun]

This is probably one of my favorite sections of long-form writing. The resources! What do you use? Recommend? What books have given you additional guidance and the topic that you think your readers should also read? What social media accounts do you follow or recommend to your readers? How can they get further help? Are there courses? Who can they reach out to if they want to know more?

Interested in [topic, content, noun]? Read [Supporting Post]: [include hyperlink for reference]

Closing / Conclusion

Time to wrap it up! Close with a key takeaway and a quote you want them to walk away with. Share one more bit of insight if you're able, along with any other links they should check out.

CALL-TO-ACTION

What do you want the reader to do next? Should they sign up for your email list? Get a free download? Get a workbook to help them with the topic? This is where you get your email signups! You've given your reader *so much information* and now you're offering them something even more—a downloadable, lead-generating piece of content! All for free.

Every single piece of content you write and design should have a clear call to action and a lead magnet attached to it to increase your email list and give you the ability to provide endless value to your readers.

If you write 2000+ words and leave your readers wondering what to do next, you're not doing your job. You're not writing for your health—you're writing and educating, leading, creating—because this is the lifestyle you chose, and it's your job!

Make sure that your call to action is clear and specific.

For instance, if you want more comments, use a CTA like "what do you think? Let us know in the comments". If you want readers to download a content upgrade, use a phrase like "download this cheat-sheet to boost your ROI by 20%".

Other Long-Form Content Tips

Use High-Quality, Relevant Images. Visuals are going to assist in telling or supporting your story. You could also follow the classic "show, don't tell" approach authors often follow in writing fiction. For example, don't say "It was raining outside." Instead, go with "Tiny droplets bounced against the asphalt, pooling into plate-sized splashes of bright mirrors against the night sky." See the difference? You're creating visuals with your words, and you can add visuals that support what you're trying to convey. You can add styled stock images, landscapes, portraits, graphics, or charts to support your writing. I have a plethora of recommendations for images beyond the free ones you'll find all over the internet, which tend to get overused (and tiresome for readers).

Also, avoid making claims without backing them up. Providing outgoing links to material that backs up your statements. Authoritative writing requires an element of backing up your claims with facts and not opinions, unless you specify that it is your opinion.

In effect, this focus on does two things:

- **Increases trustworthiness:** readers are more likely to trust web pages that reference sources of data.
- **Boosts SEO:** Google is a user of

the Hilltop algorithm (related to document search) to find relevant documents as part of a larger search algorithm. Pages that act as "hubs" and link out to a lot of sources are given higher priority in rank than pages without outbound links. Linking out to sources can have a positive impact on your rankings.

Embed Interactive Content. Embedded tweets, YouTube videos, Instagram posts, polls, quizzes, Giphy images, etc. are all genius ways to add something fun and interactive—humorous even—to your page or post. This also increases the overall amount of time the reader spends on your website. You want your reader clicking around, and playing with your content—but most importantly, subscribing.

ONE LAST THING...

You could keep your suggested blog posts all text-based, but sometimes it's much more fun to use images. If you need help with designing leaderboard ads (where you'll put your suggested images to check out other posts), or ways to make things more visual on your website in your blog post, check out my shop and look for "leaderboard templates" under the Canva templates section. Visit shop.kerrielegend.com for more information.

SO YOU HAVE THE OUTLINE, and now you're going to

get some help with writing headlines and using that article along with the subheader content to create pins. Plus, I'll give you some resource tools to help the process. It's headline writing time for Pinterest, baby.

Pinning Long-Form Content to Pinterest - Pin Creation and Design

Now that you have your remarkable, meaty content piece written and you're ready to publish, you're now ready to create your Pinterest pins. Because you spent the time carefully outlining your content and contemplating the end goal, this part is going to be super easy for you. Or, at least, with a little practice, it'll become easy with time and effort.

You're going to create 60 images based on this pillar content. 60 images from this one post. Now before you freak out, this is going to be super easy. And I have some free templates for Pinterest you can use right here:

kerrielegend.com/pinterest-templates-amplification-book

Remember all those subheaders you made in your post? You're going to use those to pose questions and garner excitement for your Pinterest pins. This is Pinterest headline writing 101!

USE UNEXPECTED HEADLINES. Catchy headlines jump out at readers because they often use unexpected words.

For example, "50 Insanely Easy Ways to Triple Your Email List" is more appealing than "50 Ways to Increase Your Email List."

Looking up synonyms for common words can be the best way to come up with eye-catching words. Get in the habit of using Thesaurus.com or Synonymy.com to find more appealing words for your headlines.

You're going to be creating 60 or so different headlines for each Pinterest image you create, so using these tools like Thesaurus and Synonymy are going to come in handy. I also have over 700 email headlines in Email Marketing Magic that you can check out, as well.

An Example. Let's say that your blog article is titled "10 Ways to Spread More Cheer this Holiday Season" and you give pointers on being the designated cheermeister, why it's important, who needs it, etc. (Yes, I know this is a silly sort of thing to write about, but you'll get the point.)

So your outline might look like something like this for your blog post:

1. Why spreading cheer is important this holiday season
2. What you can be cheerful about
3. Who needs cheer the most
4. How to spread cheer effectively
5. Avoiding the Grinch—yes or no?
6. Stealers of cheer and joy—solitude and unhealthy habits

7. Overcoming lack of cheer

8. Holiday cheer-worthy events to plan

9. When to spread cheer in your neighborhood—not at 5 a.m.

10. 10 easy ways to spread cheer without spending a fortune

11. Other ways to spread cheer if feeling generous and charitable

12. Spreading joy post-season and other non-holiday cheer-worthy things to celebrate

13. Final tips for adding cheer into your holidays

14. Closing and conclusion—the summary of all things cheer-related

15. Download your cheer list right now—the call the action

CREATE QUESTIONS **from Headline and Subheaders.** What you're going to do is create about **20 pins that have questions** posed on the Pinterest pin related to your post. For example:

1. Feeling a lack of cheer this holiday season? Here's how to get it back.

2. Need tips to spread more cheer and joy?

3. What's to be cheerful about this holiday season? This list will help you spread more cheer right away.

4. Feeling generous? Here are 10 ways to spread cheer with your favorite charities.

…and so on. You can spin intrigue with questions based on your long-form blog post because you have enough content there to talk about several different points. Starting to see how by creating a long-post you can get more out of it for Pinterest? Yeah!

CREATE CLEVER STATEMENT **or Motivating Headlines.** Clever or motivating headlines that encourage the Pinterest user to take action can really make or break your overall Pinterest strategy. Over time, you'll figure out what works better for you for click-throughs than others. By creating more Pinterest images with headlines, you enable additional testing and more presence that leads back to your pillar content.

You're going to create about 20-30 clever headlines based off of your pillar content and outline. For example:

1. Get 10x More Cheer Happening in Your Life NOW!

2. 10 Clever Ways for Spreading Epic Cheer

3. 10 Cheer-worthy Celebrations to Bring More Joy

4. This Holiday Needs YOU, Cheermeister!

…and so on.

You'll become a better headline writer in no time when you start practicing writing for Pinterest. If you need more headline inspiration or help, definitely check out Email Marketing Magic or Copy Cocktail for headline writing tips and examples, along with ways to tighten up your writing through using your unique voice. This is a skill that evolves with practice, and you'll notice your ability to come up with better headlines will speed up over time.

CREATE MOCKUP OR SCREENSHOT IMAGES **with Call to Action.** The last set of pins you're going to create are the mockups or screenshot sneak peek images of your blog post's call to action. So in the example above with "10 Ways to Spread More Cheer this Holiday Season", you could create a downloadable list of all 10 ways to spread more cheer with more details than what the blog post offers. Or, you could create an even bigger list of 25, 50, or even 100 ways to spread more cheer and offer that as a downloadable content upgrade to grow your email list.

In essence, what you're doing is offering a preview or a teaser of what the reader could get from you if they click through.

Create anywhere between 10-20 (depending on how many clever headline posts you created—60 pins total is not a scientific, firm number, but it's a number I found to be useful for testing) mockup or sneak peek screenshot Pinterest posts with a call to action associated with it. These work great for the audience type that loves downloading content in exchange for their email address.

Granted, you're going to come across a lot of freebie hoarders who will download and unsubscribe right away after they get something from you, but I've discovered a lot of wonderful customers from offering content upgrades, too, who have become loyal fans and repeat buyers from my Pinterest traffic.

There's an entire population on Pinterest, though, who are inspired to take action just from a photo (mockup) or screenshot of what they're about to receive. The word "free" is one of the top searched words on Pinterest, after all, and you'll find a lot of people who are interested in trying new things. A great way to get discovered, really.

Here's an example of a more shoppable-type pin that has a few pages embedded on the pin for a preview.

Here's another example of a pin with a mockup for a free checklist I offer on Pinterest.

So you're offering a headline of what it is, but then offering either a mockup image, a screenshot, or a teaser / preview of what the download looks like. You'll get much higher conversion for click-throughs to your site with this kind of pin.

Want to switch things up a bit? Your entire Pinterest pin image could be a mockup with no headline, too. Something to test if you're curious about whether your product can sell on it's own just based on the cover...

Modifying Your Content for Multiple URLs

Pinterest doesn't want to have a ton of traffic, all at once, leading to the same URL. So you're going to create modified content or additional content off of your pillar content piece, and the collection of pins you create for all your micro content that supports your pillar content, along with the pins from your pillar content will be scheduled over time (but sent to your tribes in a specific manner—see chapter 2).

So you have those 60 pins you just created, they are now ready to be uploaded to Pinterest or Tailwind. But before you hit publish on all the pins and upload to Pinterest or Tailwind it's important to know how to schedule these pins correctly.

The last thing you want is for Pinterest to label you and your account as a spam. That's why it's important not to push too many pins to the same URL all at once.

So refer to the Tribal Method and Image Interval Method

prior to uploading and scheduling. It'll save you a lot of headaches and do all of this more efficiently.

And because you want as much visibility and clicks to your website so you can start growing your blog while building internal links throughout your website, you need to create variations of your pillar content. Hence, the importance for modifying your pillar content to create multiple URLs so you don't get hit with a spam violation within their algorithm. Too much traffic or pins to one URL in a short timespan will get you slapped with an account closure.

What you're going to do is create "micro" content or "cluster" content based off of your pillar content you just wrote. Those 60 pins you just created serve that one blog post. Imagine if you had 10-20 spinoffs of that content based on what you initially wrote. The micro content doesn't need to be as long, but I've seen top bloggers create additional macro or long-form posts based off of their initial pillar content quite beautifully.

And the best thing, is it works.

"But I already just wrote this massive 2000-word blog post, Kerrie!" Yeah, welcome to blogging! The work isn't done. And this is why a love for writing becomes important. If you hate writing, you might have chosen the wrong path in becoming a blogger. So let's get to work!

These cluster pieces or micro pieces of content that point back to your pillar content provide additional pinned image opportunities, increase your internal links between your posts and pages, and boost your email list count.

So if you recall, you have a ton of different subheaders in your outline, and you can use some of the headlines you made on your initial Pinterest images to come up with new headlines for supporting micro content.

This is how to do it!

Creating Micro Content Using Pillar Content Pieces

Now that you have your pillar long-form post or page created, you're going to create micro content to bring even more traffic to your site, because you'll have additional pinning opportunities for each sub-article you create, pointing to the pillar content long-form article you just wrote.

Each subheader topic becomes the new core topic for a new blog post. Think of this as "base of the mountain" content—stuff you can create on a weekly or daily basis—like blogs, videos, how-to's, etc. These articles serve as hiking steps, per se, to your pillar content, or your peak of the mountain. You could have dozens, hundreds, or thousands of base content

You can also use this subcontent to fill the resource area on your pillar content page to give your readers additional reading material to digest, as well as to see what is the most popular from a click status. You'll be pointing them to your most valuable aspects of your website—focused material, and abundance of quality writing.

When coming up with subcontent ideas for your pillar content, think about what a reader might google

TIP: Think of potential subtopic content ideas in the form of a question because people usually type search queries in the form of a question. Monthly search volume for a subtopic should be between 10 and 400.

Worth Considering - Gated vs. Ungated Content

Gated and ungated content both have their pros and cons. Here's what you need to know before picking a format:

- **SEO:** When you're putting in all this work writing and creating content, you want to make sure you are fun. If you gate your content, the search engine spiders can't access it. This means you get fewer SEO benefits from it. So take that into consideration before you gate your landing page or posts. For example, I have gated content on my website that only my Patreon members get to access. It's protected. But they're plenty of content on my site for non-members to read that attract the search engine spiders now.
- **Leads:** because it's exclusive and only available to people who sign up, gated content will attract more sign ups compared to unrated content. But, a lot of

readers will bounce right off your page without signing up if it's gated. Some people just want to *read*. Consider having other articles of value they might be interested in listed in the event that they're not ready to sign up just yet.

- **Lead quality:** You're going to get fake information, and people who unsubscribe the minute they get what they want out of you. *I know, it's crappy for people to do that.* In fact, in Email Marketing Magic, I show you a prime example of what you're going to encounter. Your lead quality will suffer. And it's a waste of time if you don't have a way to score your leads and give your leads with a higher rank more value. Don't waste your time with low-ranking leads. *You have better things to do with your time!*

Conclusion

Now you know who to write pillar content and where to get your micro content ideas from, which will keep you busy writing and your editorial calendar full. You'll create 60 pins, per this methodology plan, and sprinkle them out on your feed over time, delivering a constant stream of traffic to your page or post, and that enables you to find out which pinned images work the best, along with the keyword and headlines.

This is one of the best ways to start your own research data mine so that you can start creating more of what works for your brand and set yourself apart from the rest of the pack.

Now, it's time to learn how to pin all these great images, and also learn how to efficiently schedule everything, so that your pins get to the right kind of audience right away, and that you don't get marked for spam. You might think that creating 60 images for each post takes a lot of time—it actually doesn't, when you have the right tools in place! I'll give them to you...

Chapter 2, Tribal Method and Chapter 3, Image Interval Method will go over how to get your pins to the right audience and also how to schedule with intervals. Let's get to it!

2 TRIBAL METHOD

THE TRIBAL METHOD INVOLVES A "TRIBE" approach to awareness of your pins, which involves a collection of people dedicated to Pinterest who actively pin and re-pin others' content.

Because this will be useful (and free to you), be sure to sign up for a free Tailwind account if you haven't already here. You'll get a free month on me, and you'll be able to follow along with everything I mention in this chapter.

Part of amplifying your Pinterest account is getting it in front of the right people who have boards similar to yours, as well as audiences similar to yours, who are interested in your pin. Instead of "waiting" for your pin to be discovered by the Pinterest search process, you're getting your pins on relevant boards *faster*. And, there's a higher probability that they'll be discovered with niche tribe boards available in Tailwind.

I used the tribal method as part of my strategy in growing my Pinterest account to over 14+ million monthly viewers. I wouldn't say it was a dominating part of my overall Pinterest success, as you theoretically could climb to 10+ million monthly viewers and get conversions without it, but I will say it was just as equally vital as the other methods discussed in this book. Going to the tribes with my pins got my pins on other boards that were relevant to the audience I was searching for. And because I belong to tribes that are highly curated for content, using this method helped me communicate and organize content with other bloggers, and also helped me make some virtual friends.

Tribes are powerful for pinners. This dynamic collective of pinners are the first ones who will share and redistribute your pins and content to their own audiences. You can use the tribal method in two ways: the tribes feature in Tailwind, and group boards. Tribes in Tailwind is a module feature that has become quite popular among bloggers. Tribes have become much more powerful than group board collectives, simply because the curation and the requirement of following a set of rules are more clearly defined than most group boards. It's just the nature of the setup that distinguishes the success of tribes over that of group boards.

Let's first talk about the value of being a part of tribes in Tailwind (or a tribe feature within any authorized pinning scheduler you might use), and then I'll show you how tribes are constructed and how to effectively use them.

Using a tribal method is going to help you 1) have relevant

content in your feed for your audience 2) reach an audience already conditioned and qualified for your types of pins and 3) build blogger relationships. All of these things play into building your platform on Pinterest and establish a solid upward growth pattern instead of one that is constantly up and down. Once you reach over 10 million in monthly views, you'll start to level off, because the total of population of active Pinterest users is only so many, and you'll have an active fraction of that population paying attention and engaging with your pins.

Relevant Content

Showing relevant content works both ways. One from the content that YOU are being shown as well as the content that you show in your feed to your own audience. Both are equally important. Because without relevant content streaming your way, you won't have other pins to share other than your own. And when you don't share relevant pins to your board audiences, they'll lose interest and either unfollow your or not engage (share, save, click through) your pins.

Getting relevant content at your fingertips is not just going to help you give your audience what they want and need, but you and your audience will have the *"first look"* at that content and it will save you time searching for it. Receiving everything new in your feed is quite the content treasure. And, using a tribal method of curating content just for you and your audience is a huge time saver. Time is a limited resource, after all, so using it wisely as you're growing and marketing is key.

Joining tribes on Tailwind is going to be a huge time-saver from a content relevance standpoint. You'll have first access to content that you're already looking for, and bloggers are uploading new pins related to your blogging topic every single hour of the day. You're going to find bloggers you know you can rely on for excellent blog article content, and at the same time, bloggers that only skim the surface. Because of this, Tailwind has built in a feature that allows you to checkmark the blogger pins you want to see and uncheck the ones you do not.

Relevant—but is it Good?

Some interesting revelations regarding content quality came forward after I reached the 14 million monthly views in February 2018. I started testing pin image quality and content for a "what works, what doesn't" research plan. I'll reveal my discoveries in a little bit, but first, let's back up a bit and frame up this research for you.

When you've been blogging and writing as long and as much as I have, and with enough intense focus on Pinterest, you'll start to recognize good pinning content from bad pinning content.

You want the best for your audience, right? So you need to be selective with the "relevant" content you share. Within tribes are people who will push out a lot of "crap" content that is mostly affiliate links for products they don't even use, but know they can make a buck off of. Some are disguised with beautiful pins. Others are buried within 20 or so pins uploaded to the tribes module within a matter of a few hours. You don't want to just pin anything or everything that is relevant.

I know bloggers that recommend a certain blog hosting provider because they have an affiliate program, but actually use another hosting provider altogether. I know bloggers that recommend using Tailwind and blog a lot about using tribes and other paid features, but aren't paying members and don't actually have access to those paid features. It's not exactly ethical blogging.

Take the time to read the article. Is it useful information, or is it an ad guised as a blog post article?

In time, you'll start to recognize blog posts that are just an ad for something. Typically written by a blogger whose entire mission is to make money off of affiliate income. Now, I have no beef with using affiliate links to make a few bucks here and there. But bloggers who ONLY put out content if it'll make them a buck or who don't actually use the product they're promoting have no business being rewarded traffic in your feed. They're purely there to sell. And you certainly don't want to be pitching endless ad blog posts to your audience, so you're going to want to find better content to share. It might be relevant, but it might not be good content to share.

The other type of blog posts to watch out for within tribes is the post that barely scratches the surface and reads like it was written for SEO... badly. Or they might have used a word generator to lift (steal) a blog post from another blogger and used an online word generator to "rewrite" the article just to garner website traffic.

The reason why I'm sharing this cautionary information about relevant, quality content sharing is because after I reached that 14 million monthly viewers mark and stayed there in February 2018, I started testing content quality from both the pin image and blog post point of view. I found that content that only skimmed the surface or didn't dig deeper (lack of long-form blog post mentioned in chapter 1) didn't get as many re-shares as content with long form, deeper information did. In addition, I found that while the content may be relevant and quality, if the pin image wasn't super pretty to look at, it wasn't re-pinned.

So it's definitely worth the time to read the article prior to sharing. Just because the pin is pretty doesn't mean that the content is relevant or quality. You certainly don't want to abuse your followers' trust in following you, so be sure to only share the good stuff that is worth sharing in your eyes.

Look for bloggers who routinely post long-form content and have blog posts that don't pitch a paid affiliate link product all the time. You'll find higher quality content with these kinds of bloggers. And they do exist in all sorts of niches. You just have to take the time to vet them out and make a "list" of sorts to include them on your tribe re-pinning plan.

I have a list of bloggers I specifically look for, and will go into my tribes and clear out everyone and just checkmark their profile so I can share all of their new stuff. They've built enough trust with me so I know I can just spot check from time to time to make sure what I'm sharing is good for my audience. And this is a process that I recommend (spot-checking) because from time to time, bloggers change direction and maybe the content they once used to blog about is no longer going in the same direction you and your own audience is looking for.

For example, a blogger that gives great tips about YouTube and whose entire platform is pro-YouTube who decides to switch to self-hosted Vimeo, and has shown signs they're abandoning their YouTube presence. You'll have to make the decision, if you're blogging about YouTube, whether or not that new direction is one you want to share with your readers. Your choice!

Support bloggers who offer checklists, resource guides, courses, etc. by pinning their content and give your audience a steady stream of pins with that kind of quality content provided it's relevant. Those kinds of materials take a lot of time to create and roll out, and there's nothing wrong with supporting other bloggers who could be construed as your "competitors". They're just going to challenge you to dig deeper and raise the bar on what kind of content is already out there.

Reach Highly Receptive Audiences

Receptive audiences are built by commonalities in content. By sharing each other's relevant content, everybody in your tribe benefits from additional exposure to each other's like-minded audiences. This is why you have to be selective about the tribes you join. You don't want to join them all or even "free for all" tribes. You definitely want the tribes you join to be relevant to your audience.

When I talk about an audience that is pre-qualified, I mean an audience that is already interested in a specific niche or topic. For example, let's say you blog about travel in Brazil. Tribe members are pre-qualified for your pins if they belong to a tribe that focuses on travel in South America, or travel in general. The more specific the tribe is, the more finely curated content you'll find.

Pre-qualified lists are curated everywhere—people who have recently moved, own their home vs. rent, are of a specific age, have a subscription to a certain magazine, etc. When you pre-qualify your audience to people already interested in what you blog about or offer, you are further targeting an audience that is going to be receptive to your message and products / services, making conversion easier, and less costly from an ad campaign viewpoint.

You're going to find tribes who only talk about or allow content about interior design. Specific pins like food recipes or housing / renting companies are forbidden. And those rules are clearly stated in the tribe description. The reason for that is the tribe owner wants to have highly-curated pins for similar bloggers to choose from. Having irrelevant content within the tribe feed is hugely annoying, and that's why you can get booted out of tribes for infringing on those established rules.

There are also free-for-all tribes, which I think are a bad idea with the exception of the possibility of discovery by an audience of bloggers that wouldn't normally find you given your kind of search terms, keywords or other tribes you might belong to. Free-for-all tribes have a myriad of different kinds of pins from Disney trips and baby gear to high-end real estate and financial advising. From college advice to beer mugs. So you never know what is going to come out of those tribes— could be anything!

If you're going to join a free-for-all tribe just for the exposure, know that it's not something that I would recommend from a time investment perspective simply because it takes too long to search for posts and pins that would be relevant to your audience. In addition, for each pin you share, you have to share someone else's, as per most tribe rule descriptions. Your time is more valuable. You might not find anything relevant. It may be better just to leave the tribe than to invest time into something that isn't already curated for your audience and feed.

I have left several tribes for various reasons. Some I left because the tribe wasn't managed well and allowed a lot of crap content to be pinned (no descriptions, non-working links, Instagram posts, banner-type small images, direct affiliate links to non-related products, stolen pin content, etc.).

When you belong to a highly-receptive, pre-qualified tribe audience, you're increasing the likelihood that your pins will be shared, your blog posts will be read, and your email list will increase with pre-qualified people, who are already interested in the topic you're talking about. This means that you're going to have higher click rates and opens on your emails when they subscribe—because they're actually interested in what you have to say about that topic!

So now you can see why having a receptive, pre-qualified audience really matters not just from a sharing perspective, but how much easier it'll be on you with your email marketing efforts and product alignment for conversion to that specific audience.

Build Trusted Relationships with Bloggers and Your Audience

Tribes has the potential to be a marketing asset that's as powerful and durable as your email list, because of your ability to tap other bloggers with similar audiences as well as build relationships with your audience that might not have been possible without using that feature module.

Tribes in Tailwind now has the feature where you can see who is re-pinning your pins to their boards. There's a lot more accountability and transparency on the tribes module than there was before, which is nice, because now you can thank the bloggers who are sharing your content and take note of who is not. This can ultimately help you make the decision whether to share another blogger's content if they're not sharing yours.

Tribes also has a messenger chat app built in so you can send messages back and forth to other bloggers. It's a nice feature to have in place for a quick "thanks" and introduction-type messages.

I have used it to work out post exchanges and guest blogging opportunities with other bloggers, including other brands. You can use it to make requests of other bloggers or let them know you just finished a post that you're really excited about, and ask for them to share it with their audience in exchange for something. Or, for paid products created by other bloggers, you can always request (not expect) either a trial copy or a free copy to blog or endorse it on your own blog. It's a great way to build relationships with other bloggers.

From an audience viewpoint, you're building trust with your audience by fulfilling your brand promise. By providing your audience with content they've come to expect from you. Imagine if all of a sudden I started about blogging about goats and cupcakes on my blog. That'd be weird. My audience would probably freak out..

So tribes is going to help you discover other bloggers that your audience may be able to learn from or may want to follow along with your blog, as well. By recommending and supporting other bloggers, you're only positioning yourself as a secure, confident blogger who's not afraid of sharing the limelight with others equally as talented. There will be a time and a place for exclusivity and unique control over internally-developed content. When you're ready. But until then, be sure to share others and show your confidence. It only builds trust and respect from your audience.

Say "thanks" and communicate with your fellow tribe pinners. It's a module designed to bring fellow-minded people together and share content. And a little gratitude goes a long way with these kinds of bloggers.

Vibrant Community of Dedicated Pinners

Think of marketing on Pinterest like a pie. I spend 1/3 of my time creating content via writing, 1/3 of my time creating images, and 1/3 of my time within Tailwind tribes, actively engaging by uploading my own content and sharing content created by others.

There are about 20,000 Tailwind members who have access to tribes. There are a ton of niches and topics within the tribes modules that are broken down by topic. Within each category there are more defined tribes that may further a niche down to a more specific topic. For example, interior design as a category may have tribes specific for tiny house interior design or man-cave interior design.

Some tribes are more success than others. That's where looking at the tribe activity level will help you decide whether or not to request to join the tribe.

Because I value my time and I know you do, too, I don't bother joining or requesting access to tribes that don't have 4 bars or more, unless I know that it's comprised of some pretty big blogger names and is brand new. You can kind of see who is part of the tribe by looking at the people you might already know based on other tribes you're in. You could also give a tribe a whirl and if it doesn't seem like it's working out, you can always leave. Just remember that when you leave a tribe, your pins in the tribe disappear. So be sure not to use joining/leaving tribes to gain exposure as a strategy because that will backfire quickly and all the time you spent adding pins to tribes will be gone.

But do leave tribes that aren't performing well or are mismanaged. Leave tribes that seem overly demanding of your time. For example, say you're in the process of uploading and scheduling 60 or so pins to tribes and if a tribe owner threatens to boot you out if you don't re-share others pins 1:1 that particular day.

Leave. Immediately. It's a given that big bloggers need a few more days to get caught up. If you're a bigger account than the tribe owner, they should be thanking you up and down for being a part of their tribe, because it's your reach and sharing that makes a difference. And if you have a tribe owner with a relatively small account (less than 1 million monthly views) it's probably not worth your time anyway trying to appease their demands. (Hint—look for tribes with a bigger reach and more followers than you have.)

To offset or prevent that situation of a deficit from happening altogether, if you know that you're in a great tribe and things are working out for you sharing-wise, then try sharing others' pins in bulk. You can start by taking it tribe by tribe and get ahead of the pack with more shares than what you've contributed to the group.

This will prevent any sharing deficits (red zone). Here's an example of a tribe I'm in where I'm in the red zone at the moment of image snap. You can see on Striving Bloggers I have a pin deficit running next to the activity level icon. The tribes module shows two columns: pins you've uploaded and shared, and pins you've shared created by others.

Red zone means you have a deficit running and you could be risking your tribe member status in that particular tribe. You'll want to get that cleared up as quickly as you can so you don't get scolded by the tribe owner, or worse, kicked out without warning.

What constitutes great results within Tailwind tribes? Well, that largely depends on your kind of blog and how you define success. However, knowing how to interpret the numbers within tribes will give you better insight into how each tribe is performing, and whether or not you should continue being a part of a specific tribe.

Because you have to weigh both time investment or the cost (using that 1/3 of your time marketing wisely) and the benefit. Do the benefits outweigh the cost? Are those re-shares and re-pins getting you conversions? Because that's the ultimate goal, right? Getting the right customers who will buy from you?

There's a few numbers to take into consideration as you're making any sort of success determination within tribes. This screenshot of the side panel of the tribe community shows the stats of the group as a whole as well as your own specific stats related to that tribe group.

Re-shares shows the number of times that your tribemates have shared your content. Re-pins means the number of re-pins generated from the re-shares of your content. So by from 403 re-shares, I got 65 re-pins to non-tribemember boards. Reach means the potential number of impressions on Pinterest from all the re-shares of the content. Keep in mind, it's the potential impressions, not actual.

The tribe overview gives you insight on the re-shares and re-pins. This basically gives you idea of the health of the tribe you're a member of. How strong are the accounts of the members who have joined the tribe?

Bear in mind, members with huge Pinterest accounts (like mine) influence that number greatly. So the number I see is the strength of the other members not including my own. This is why you want to find tribes with members who have a bigger following and reach than your own Pinterest account may have.

One of the ways I found success during my months of testing between December 2018 and February 2019 was to get featured on weekly highlights within the tribes module. This is what that looks like:

Weekly highlights gives you the run-down of who has been super busy within tribes, sharing others' content pieces and pins, and you can see their own submissions in the orange outlined boxes. Then, you can also see the most re-shared pins of the week. I've been featured a few times in both areas for having popular pins that went "viral". This is just a side effect of putting out quality content and being an active participant within the tribal module.

Effortless Collaboration

Tailwind is going to help you team up with other bloggers a lot easier. No more complicated spreadsheets of who shared what and who you could partner up with. No more sharing threads or pin-for-pin groups on Facebook that aren't even relevant to your audience. No more email chains with bloggers begging for exposure and guest blog posting opportunities or brand partnering.

This can all be done within Tailwind tribes. It's simple. There's messaging built in. You can keep things much more casual until it's contract time. This is a module tool that was built for marketers to network together and share content. And it's effortless.

Group Boards

Now that we've covered Tailwind tribes, let's discuss group boards. Group boards used to be "the thing" back when BoardBooster was alive and well. Group boards played a bigger role back in 2017 and 2018 than they do now. Group boards allowed people to curate content on shared boards together (like tribes, only no real oversight or data), and share from those group boards to each pinner's own audience.

Some Pinterest users are still in the mindset that group boards are still the rave. They're actually not, if you look at all the improvements and modifications that Pinterest has made just in 2019. Pinning to your own boards and focusing more on quality long-tail keywords, developing those lead magnets and opting for long-form blog posts instead of short ones filled with affiliate links is a much better game plan than seeking out group boards.

So if you're still thinking that you need to join a ton of group boards to be successful, please put down that knife and get current. What's more important is getting your content in front of a pre-qualified audience, and in a controlled setting like Tailwind tribes, that can be achieved much more effectively.

Do I still belong to group boards? Yes. Do I still pin to group boards? Yes. But it's not a big part of my strategy. I put my group boards at the bottom of my Pinterest profile, because it's not groups that have made my success on Pinterest. It was quality content (lots of it, really, used strategically) and focusing on the methods described in this book.

Basic Tailwind Tribes Knowledge

Getting started. On the left side of the Tailwind panel, you'll see three little icon dudes grouped together. That's your tribe module. Click on it, and it'll take you to your tribe dashboard, or "https://www.tailwindapp.com/dashboard/tribes".

Find your tribes. If you're new to tribes, you can click on the button "Find a Tribe". f you click on it a search window will open up and you will be able to look for tribes by keywords or categories, or if you already know the name of the tribe that you would like to join you can look for it. There you can go into the categories area and drill down into there.

After you type in a keyword a list of tribes will appear that are relevant to your search. Each tribe will list out the level of activity, some basic information such as name, description and rules.

Size of tribe matters. Bigger tribes give you more content to choose from and a bigger audience for your pins. At the same time, in a smaller tribe your content is more likely to be chosen for re-pinning. You have to weigh the size of the tribe with the amount of reach each of those members have. Don't worry—if you join a tribe that gives you less favorable data than the basic upfront before joining or requesting to join, you can always leave the tribe.

On the right side of the tribe summary you can see if you are already a member of the tribe (handy if you belong to a lot of them).

Open tribes vs. closed tribes. Some tribes are open to the public and if they are, the only thing you need to do is to click on "join tribe" and you are in. I'm a member of the PowerUp so I can belong to a LOT of tribes. Some of the tribes are listed as join by request only. This means that you have to ask to join and then, if the owner of the tribe thinks that you are a good fit for their tribe they will approve your request. While you wait, you'll be using one of your limited tribe requests, which limits the number of tribes you can request to join at once. You can have a maximum of 5 pending requests and Tailwind keeps the count for you, if you're not a PowerUp user. If you're a PowerUp user, that number goes to a limit of 10 tribe requests.

Keep it to your niche. Only join tribes related to your blog's niche. Remember that your goal is to get your pins out there and shared. Not to spam tribes that have no interest in what you're sharing. It's a great way to get booted out and build a negative reputation in the online community.

For example, if you add a pin about CBD oil (I see this a lot) to a tribe that talks about interior design, you'll get a re-pin rate of zero, get kicked out of the tribe, and make a not-so-nice name for yourself. So don't do that.

Choose your tribes carefully. When choosing your tribes, keep in mind that you'll need to share pins from other members so try to stay as close to the topics of your boards as possible. If you initially see a lot of pins in a free-for-all type of tribe community that you just wouldn't share with your crowd, consider leaving.

Use the Chrome or Safari extension. You can add the Tailwind Chrome extension to make things go super fast for adding pins to your tribe module. It's my number one recommendation for efficiency in pinning and scheduling, as well as sharing to tribes. As of the date of publication, the Safari extension has a bit of a bug in it. It deletes the link and description from the pin if you're pinning from Pinterest, and allows the user to submit their own link and put their own description in the pin. I think that this has led to a lot of "stolen pin" accusations that may have been unwarranted based on how easy it is to bulk schedule and run a macro for pin descriptions and links, like I tend to use. (Yes, there are macros you can run in your browser to streamline these kinds of things, speeding up your marketing process without violating terms of service.)

Follow the rules. Usually, tribes work with a ratio of 1:1. This means that for each pin you add to the tribe panel you should share one. Tailwind will keep track of how many you've shared and submitted, as illustrated by a screenshot I shared with you earlier. So don't panic and think you need to create an elaborate spreadsheet for all of this. Not worth it. Tailwind will give you all the data you need.

Find your content. Additionally, the same toolbar where you can check your ratio also offers additional features:

Use the search bar. At the top of your tribe dashboard, regardless of which tribe you're working in, you'll see a bar at the top that will give you some data, viewing options, and search opportunities.

All–This will show you all pins in that tribe.

New–This will only show you pins that have been added since your last visit.

Yours–This will show you only your pins you've added to the tribe.

Skipped–Here are all the pins that you have skipped. You can skip pins that you know you won't schedule to make your stream less cluttered. This is especially helpful if you've got a lot of spam activity going on within the tribe. You can essentially block out by pin or by the author of the pin in the member list panel.

Screen the content feed by member. I tend to screen members and block out members I know don't write or produce great content my audience would be interested in. So use the member panel and only re-pin content that is quality. Pin stuff you wish you would have written or created yourself!

Numbers aren't everything. Don't pin a pin just because it has high numbers. I've seen pins getting a high re-pin rate that don't even have a working link behind them or even a decent blog post written. Check the accuracy of the link, and don't rely on the numbers alone. Do your own scope.

Use the hide button. Don't show pins that you've already scheduled. (This plays into my strategy in the next section of this chapter.) Once you share, your scheduled pin will be tagged. The green one says "Published" that means that you've already pinned that pin on one of your boards. The blue one says "Scheduled" which means that that pin is already in your queue to be pinned. You're still able to pin them again, but I would try to avoid re-pinning the same things. You can hide these altogether by clicking on the checkbox in the bar.

Pin efficiently. So you know I use the Chrome extension to quickly schedule pins from Pinterest, but I also schedule them from the Tailwind tribes, as well. I have a course that goes over this in detail so you can be the fastest pinner in the West, and you can check that out if you'd like here. But the fastest way is not to just use the Chrome extension, but to schedule in bulk by board category.

I use the "save to drafts" feature and keep one board in mind while I'm adding pins to schedule and share from my tribes boards. It's the fastest method I've found and keeps my marketing and sharing time down to a minimum, leaving that saved time to create more content and design more products for my shop.

The Strategy to 14+ Million Monthly Viewers

I use a specific strategy when using Tailwind tribes, and you're about to see why it works over what you might typically see happening on the tribe boards.

A few things first to set up this mindset and help you understand why this works better than what you might already be doing, though.

There are millions of users as consumers on Pinterest who do not have Pinterest business accounts. There are only around 20,000 users on Tailwind. Those that DO have Pinterest business accounts and use Tailwind, often belong to tribes, because every blogger pretty much knows that tribes is a helpful tool.

And within tribes as a module, you're going to see bloggers

that belong to several of the same tribes as you. Because of this, there is often redundancy between the tribes. You'll see the same pins being submitted on the same day by the same blogger, across 5, 20 or even 100 or so different tribes. Let's assume they're following a basic pin A/B testing strategy discussed in Pinterest Marketing: 80k to 14+ Million in 3 Months (that's a big assumption, because I only see a few bloggers actually following through with this solid approach).

With the classic A/B testing approach, a blogger will generally submit to the tribes 4 pins for the day—4 pins with 2 different images, and 2 different pin descriptions. It's their blog post for the day (or for the week). And then you won't see them pin something else (because of the 2-4 pin limit in each tribe group) until the next day or week.

That's a losing strategy. Why?

Yes, it's good to A/B test. Yes, I do it. But what's wrong with this picture?

For one, you have the same people in multiple tribes on Tailwind. Two, you have a limited number of pins you can pin to each tribe. Two, mostly, some stretch to four without getting in trouble. It's become common knowledge that pinners who take Pinterest seriously pin 4 images to one blog post. (The smart ones adopt a Pinterest Amplification strategy, which you're learning about right now.)

Three, once a tribe member schedules all four of your pins (let's hope they do!) for sharing, that's it. They're either going to hide the pins they see in another tribe you've submitted to that they've already scheduled (which means the pins you already shared in another tribe are going to be hidden in the tribe they just moved onto to share more pins) or they're going to see them tagged and not share them again. Makes sense for them to do that right? Right.

But what if you could encourage them to share more of your pins and still drive traffic to the same or a similar post? Maybe with a different pin image and different description? Yeah. That's the game plan going on here.

I pin 60 of my own domains pin daily as a part of this strategy, which supports other Pinterest Amplification methods mentioned in this book. Keep in mind, when you put them altogether, you become a powerhouse of website traffic and a professional blogger in no time at all.

This is where scheduling direct from Tailwind comes in handy. Because although you're going to schedule and pin directly to your own board on Pinterest, you don't want your account to be marked as spam, with 60 or so images going to the same URL on the same day. That'd be bad news bears. You need them spread out. You can't spread out sharing to Tailwind tribes on the module. What you share gets submitted right then and there. This is why you need to shake things up and vary your pin images to the URL or similar content (using the content modifier method) so that you get your end game plan accomplished: the conversion.

So what you do is schedule the pins from Tailwind over time, but submit all 60 pins to your tribes, varying the images over the 20, 50, 0r 80 or so tribes you might belong to. You'd pin four pins to each tribe, two with the same image but two different description, and 2 with another image, with two different descriptions. So it'd look a lot like this:

Tribe 1: image 1, image 1 with alt-description, image 2, and image 2 with alt-description

Tribe 2: image 3, image 3 with alt-description, image 4, and image 4 with alt-description

Tribe 3: image 5, image 5 with alt-description, image 6, and image 6 with alt-description

…and so on. You get the idea.

The Effect of the Tribal Method

What this does is give your tribe members more opportunities to pin your pins in various different tribes. Because it's a new or different image, you increase the probability of 1) being seen by your tribe members, 2) being pinned multiple times instead of just the four you'd normally submit and 3) increase your website traffic.

You can then find out what kind of pin is working for you. Which headlines work better than others? Did offering a screen print work better with a lead magnet than one without? Did you use a word that converted better than another?

This is data that will come back to you quicker over a period of time so that... what? You can create *more of that thing that worked.*

If a tribe member sees and shares your four pins in one tribe, they're not going to pin them again in another tribe group. But they might if they're varying images or lead to other content modified with a different URL as described in chapter 1. So why pin four of the same pins to every single tribe you belong to on the same day? Stop doing that. There's a better way.

What I discovered was that my tribe mates would re-pin my images in various tribes I belonged to if we both belonged to several of the same groups. In addition, I got back better data on what kind of headlines and pin layouts worked better, faster.

Conclusion

If you aren't quite grasping this method yet, consider enrolling in my course where you can access the live videos on how to put this all together quickly. You'll get access to watching me pin and design live, and it'll blow your mind. Hopefully not literally. I'm a big fan of efficient and cheap marketing, because time is valuable and I have an abundance of little people who eat all my food at home, and that's where the money needs to be—not paying for ads and marketing that doesn't work. So I'm making sure you learn how to do this method correctly so you can rise to the top quickly too is important to me. I want you to implement with precision and confidence!

My tribal method strategy isn't going to be for everyone. It definitely works. It doesn't take a huge amount of time when you learn how to do it efficiently. But maybe you don't want to have to pay for tribes or maybe tribes isn't your thing and you only want to create four images for your posts and move on. Whatever you choose is completely up to you. Just know that this is a solid strategy that has garnered visibility and conversion up the yin yang, so worth considering.

I'm excited to see you put this method in place and give it a try! Even if you only long-form blog one piece a week, doing it this way will be super beneficial for you.

3 IMAGE INTERVAL METHOD

THE IMAGE interval method is a necessity to learn, whether you choose to implement any other method or not. The reason? Don't get marked as spam and get your account closed like so many other bloggers have this year. Let's get into it.

Belonging to many Pinterest groups on Facebook has its benefits. Being an introvert, I get to quietly observe from a safe virtual distance all of the questions bloggers have along with some of their Pinterest pains and gains. Mostly pains, though. I don't engage; I listen. I watch. Observing, mostly, the logic that many bloggers use that lacks common sense.

And maybe you've seen some of the Pinterest-related posts on some of the groups or forums and have been curious. Some of the questions are really *really* good. Like return on investment with pinning strategies, questions about reasons for low pin engagement from one month to the next, requests for advice or information on how-to's for software, etc.

The challenge with most bloggers using Pinterest for marketing is that they don't have a clear enough understand of the tool or mechanisms behind the tool itself, and proceed to dive right in without knowing the cause and effects of each action. Most of these pains revolve around being able to publish pins on Pinterest and ultimately, getting shut down for one reason or another.

There have been a LOT of account closures in the last year, due to the preparation of Pinterest's move for an IPO (initial public offering) on the stock market, and their desire to get in compliance with federal regulations regarding misinformation with health-oriented content. Basically, they wanted things or any content claiming "healing" or "cure" that is not FDA backed to be stripped from the platform altogether, along with other questionable content with any form of regulation.

But then there are the pinners and bloggers who make complaints or voice concern about their spam-level pinning habits on the groups:

Here are a few prime examples:

"My Pinterest account just got shut down and I've filed a BBB report. They won't respond to me or re-open my account and won't tell me why."

Quietly, I mutter to myself... *"Because you were spamming your content across several boards in a short timeframe. That's why. And that's why I unfollowed you last year."* But no one likes the truth. But that's what it is. It's harsh, and real. You can't spam on Pinterest with an impatient attitude just because you need to make money fast or get a lot of page hits, thinking there aren't going to be consequences. The URLs, images, and descriptions need to be varied and balanced with the content of others mixed in.

"Pinterest isn't letting me pin anymore today and says I hit a spam limit. I'm trying to share to my group boards. How is this happening when I'm only pinning 4 new images?"

I shake my head after I look at how many group boards they belong to. *"You can't pin the same 4 images to 50 boards all pointing to the same URL and expect Pinterest to be ok with that."*

Seriously. That's the prime definition of spamming. Last one, I promise.

"I'm just not getting traffic to some of my best content even though I have great images. Even when I loop it three months later, I get crickets. What am I doing wrong?"

And that's the real question and battle that a lot of Pinterest Business users have. The problem with this issue isn't about lack of interest about the topic. It's how it's framed, presented, and the frequency of how the post is presented.

The lack of pins and testing them for one piece of content.

Diversification

Most college students are told to start saving in a 401k or establish a savings account. As you grow older, so does that nest egg. If you've ever worked with a broker on investing, you'll know one of the cardinal rules is to diversify your portfolio. *Don't put all your eggs in one basket.* You spread out your money and watch it grow (hopefully).

Right? So why would that concept be any different for pinning images to Pinterest? Would you honestly put all of your hopes and future dreams in one stock and let it ride? No. That's crazy. You'd never do that. That's an incredibly risky approach to investing.

You know what else is risky? Thinking that two images with two different headlines and descriptions is going to do it for you. It won't. It's extremely limited.

You have to **diversify** your pin images and headlines for each and every blog post. You need to create **more** pins for your content pieces so that you can arrive at better, more accurate conclusions. Draw the readers in using various headlines and test what works.

What happens, for example, if you create a pin that says "How to Make Money from Home", and it gets crickets? What's the answer? Do you just go back to the same pin and change the keywords and hashtags? Do you just create more images with the same headline 2-3 months later? No.

But that's what a lot of people marketing on Pinterest tend to do. Instead of creating more, better pins with more curious or intriguing headlines, Pinterest Business pinners have developed this notion that going back to their boards and "cleaning up" or "auditing" their Pinterest account is the answer. They'll spend a couple hundred dollars thinking that some unqualified self-proclaimed expert on Pinterest is to have the answer and fix everything.

It isn't the answer. That's a complete waste of time and money, if you want my honest opinion. And it's certainly not a cure to what IS the problem—the methodology of the user is doing.

Even with looping in place, you're taking a huge risk that that one headline on that one pin is going to bring an abundance of traffic. You could think it's a great headline. You may even think it's clever or nails the topic of your blog post or page perfectly. But what if it doesn't get conversions? In a sea of pins, you're placing all your bets on one image (or two if you're doing A/B testing regularly) and a couple of headlines.

Stop.

Remember chapter one when we talked about the reason we create 60 or so images for that one pillar piece of content? We want to give the Pinterest community ample opportunity to be triggered by one of the pins you've created. The more pins that are out there for that post, the ones that are the best-written, best-designed pins are going to rise to the top. The ones that didn't perform well will signal to you that those kinds of headlines or images didn't work for you, and your audience didn't respond to them as much as the ones that DID work.

And then you look for the commonalities between them.

This goes beyond merely refreshing pins from blog posts you wrote a year ago or even a couple years ago. While refreshing is good, keep in mind when you're doing that task you're only replacing or adding one extra image to the post. It might not be enough. Again, you're banking on that one set of headlines or a couple of images to work.

So for each piece of content you write from here on out, you'll create much more than four images. I've been doing 60 per page and post, and it has worked beautifully, giving me valuable data I need to do more of what works.

And when you use a Canva template pre-built with 60 Pinterest templates with a similar style (great for branding), this is a process that goes very quickly, and can be done in 15 minutes.

Visit shop.kerrielegend.com and search for 60 Pinterest templates so you can quickly get moving and produce images efficiently with quality design!

The Beauty is in the Scheduling

One of the tricks to this pin scheduling and blogging thing we love to do as bloggers and writers is to do things in bulk. I touched on this in Pinterest Marketing about how much time you'll save when you batch your photos. Batching everything out *will* save you time.

Tailwind is one of the few software apps I'm willing to throw money at every month. Why? It has helped changed the major process of Pinterest image upload, handles scheduling to all the boards and tribes, and keeps things organized for me.

The first step is to upload your 60 images you've created like in chapter 1's Content Modifier Method. Upload all 60 images in bulk, using Tailwind's bulk upload tool in the Publishing module.

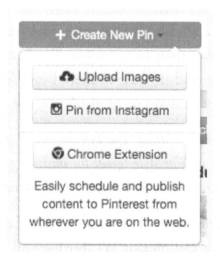

The other way you can do this, if you're not planning on using Pinterest, is to use Pinterest's built in pin builder tool. Just go up to the right-hand corner and click on "Create Pin".

From there, you can add images using the left-hand panel.

In using the pin builder, the only way adding images in bulk works is if you're creating a slideshow pin. You'll have to upload each image individually on the left. I wouldn't be surprised if Pinterest makes improvements or enhancements to the pin builder module, making it easier for people to upload more content and create ads faster. We'll see what happens in 2020…

But let's get back to Tailwind, because I think that's the appropriate tool to use for a project like this.

After you upload your 60 images, your draft board will look something like this:

If you're not completely familiar with Tailwind, know that board lists are helpful for something like this. You can group all of your group boards and boards that are related to a specific topic together. You'll see those at the top of the panel where it says "Add Board to All". This means you're going to be scheduling these pins to all the relevant boards… over time.

And now you can see that my boards have been added to the pins all at once. Using the board list feature, you can create an abundance of different groups to keep your content as relevant to the boards you're posting on.

Now, before you hit "Schedule All Drafts", we're going to do a few things first:

- Add to tribes (using my very specific tribal method)
- Add to SmartLoop
- Use interval
- Add to Queue

Add to tribes. So take your pins in order, from 1-60, and follow the tribal method of scheduling. This means that you'll be able to schedule out to 30+ tribes all in the same day, using 60 different kinds of pins. So no tribe is going to see the same pin set that another tribe you belong to is going to see. This also means that the same blogger is more likely to to schedule more than just two pins leading to the same URL.

You have the option to repeat the process and only add to tribes without re-publishing your pins to the same boards, if you want to rotate the pins throughout the tribes. Or you can always move along, going to your next piece of micro content for the next day.

The point is to spread everything out and not have so much repetition, including the scheduled pins to your own domain boards and group boards.

Add to SmartLoop. Here's an example of a set of how-to blog posts that I have set up in Tailwind.

You can see that there are 244 pins I have looping just in the how-to post category. You can set up different boards and strategies for various kinds of campaign missions. Between your new posts and your SmartLoop posts, you'll be pinning a healthy amount per day, and spreading your new pins out over time, while still getting all your new pins sent to your tribe right away.

So even though you haven't pinned a certain pin design to your brand board yet, your tribe members have already had a chance to schedule it and send traffic to your website.

Brilliance.

Set the interval. Avoid spam. Make sure you have plenty of pins already scheduled from your tribes and that you've set how many of your own pins you want to reserve for each day. This is important to do so that you're not scheduling a bunch of pins set to interval right away, all the same time. Having a semi-full queue of others' pins will help you spread them out over time.

See the "Use Interval" button in the bottom left corner? Use it!

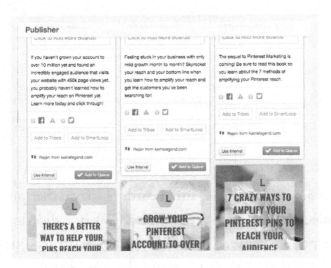

This is what will come up once you hit the interval option:

Now, you can't see *all* my boards I have the pin being scheduled to, but you get the idea. What I did during the testing period between December 2018-February 2019, and still continue to date, is to spread the pin image out using at least 1 day between boards. So over time, that 1 pin hits about

20+ different boards it's applicable to. Plus, I have all the other pin images that are going to be sent out in intervals, as well, mixed in with others' content pieces.

So by doing this, I'll be giving my audience a constant stream of content over time, leading to the same URL, without triggering the Pinterest spam algorithm, bringing traffic in nonstop while each pin image takes a hold.

Add to queue. Add your pin descriptions, hashtags, and link. Once you get your custom pin description in and check your link, you're finally ready to add the pin to the queue. Check your dashboard to make sure you got everything set up right and that the pins are loading. I typically do a quick scroll just to verify.

You'll do this 4-step process for each pin, and scheduling should only take about 30 minutes. Think of it as scheduling out your advertising well in advance—60 posts you've created goes a long way.

In search, Pinterest will help users find your material naturally. Eventually, as you create more and more headlines and evaluate which pins are getting better attention than others, you'll start to notice trends that work for you.

Conclusion

Pinning in intervals is a smart move on Pinterest. You can still pin a ton from your own domain provided that there's balance with other content. I can commit to 300 pins or more a day.

Maybe you'll choose to work up to that gradually. Maybe you'll stay at the same quantity you're at now, but will plan to change your use of intervals and add the content modifier and tribal method.

Whatever you choose to do, know that trying new things and staying committed to those changes so you can conduct testing, is going to be a beneficial move for you. If I had just stuck with what I was doing (which is what everyone else just said to do online), I would *still be fluctuating at 80k-250k monthly viewers, depending on the season)*. Change is good. Give it a whirl.

4 LANDING PAGE METHOD

YOU'VE GOT the content method, tribal method, and image interval method under your belt so far. That's awesome. But what kind of content keeps people coming back or visiting your website? How do you write content that supports all those pins as part of these methods?

This chapter is all about landing pages—what they are, the benefits of writing them, how to write landing pages that supports both long- and short-form articles, and how they'll apply to your overall Pinterest amplification plan.

Landing pages will be directly related to superior results in amplifying your reach and tapping into audiences who originally had no clue about who you are and what you offer. They are my favorite way to test out copy, images, and conversion. I hope by the end of this chapter you'll be all pumped up and jazzed to use them more. This is a longer chapter, so buckle in; we're in for a long ride with this method.

Landing pages area these magical pages on your website that take readers through your product, help them become familiar with the features and benefits, and present them with an offer. Used with Pinterest in mind, you'll be a powerhouse of a traffic and conversion.

You probably know about them, maybe you even love them, and if you're really into landing pages, you lay awake late at night thinking about them. Yeah chief, we're talking about landing pages. Those lovable digital customer sponges we obsess with optimizing, tweaking, updating, and testing.

Whether you're a blogger, author, social media guru, or virtual assistant of sorts—you'll have a healthy relationship with the landing page as both a creator and benefactor for your bottom line. Sometimes, your business might go through rough patches, or even dead zones of sales, where you wonder why we bother with them so much. But landing pages are going to work hard for you like your best employee or consultant ever, giving you much-needed data, increasing sales conversions, attracting new leads, and receiving traffic from Pinterest for offers you've worked tirelessly hard to create.

You should try to use a landing page for every inbound pin you create on Pinterest. If you're like most online marketers, you're probably creating multiple products and are running more than one promotional offer. Your home page just isn't going to cut it, and neither will sending new traffic cold turkey to a product listing with a "Buy Now" button. There's a style and flair for taking Pinterest traffic specifically and catering to the winner's interests. Your goal is to provide a relevant experience based on the pin they clicked on, which signals an interest.

The whole point of using the landing page method is to take Pinterest traffic from a relevant pin a user is interested in and turn them into customers. Bam.

Landing pages are super handy in converting Pinterest readers to immediate buyers. There's a few ways to approach pinning to landing pages or leading Pinterest users to landing pages, which are covered in this chapter later.

Most Pinterest Business users only have one or two landing pages (if they're exercising A/B testing as recommended) set up for a product. What happens if that combination of copy and layout wasn't appealing? You could be driving endless traffic to a page of copy that never converts... and you'll never know why.

Big problem.

You need **more** landing pages, not just one. And the more you have, the more pins you can create and publish over time, creating a constant stream of pinned traffic opportunities.

But first, let's go through the elements I believe are crucial to your success in using landing pages with Pinterest. Once you master landing pages, you can use them for your social media purposes, as well, like on LinkedIn, Twitter, Instagram, and Facebook, if you choose to do so.

What is a Landing Page?

Believe it or not, you visit landing pages all the time as you click around the internet on your laptop and every time you click on a professional ad on social media.

A landing page is the designated page you're taken to when you click on an ad. It's the page that follows a call-to-action button on the ad you just saw in your feed. A landing page can also sometimes serve as a homepage of sorts for a website.

It's also a web page with a specific purpose—the objective of a landing page created with Pinterest in mind is to convert pinners into customers. Online marketers While there are several types of landing pages, which I'll illustrate later, the intent is the same—get more leads and turn viewers into buyers. You most likely don't have a brick and mortar storefront, so this is how it's done on the online arena.

Pinterest pins created for your landing pages like we did in chapter 1 with the content modifier method will lead thousands of people to your various landing pages, no matter the type you use.

In fact, you can use landing pages of different kinds to figure out what the users of Pinterest like buying from so you can start creating more of what works. After all, Pinterest is the best place to test things out before launching, and big name brands are only just starting to figure that out. I've known this for years!

So *you'd be right* if you're thinking that lead magnets like checklists and cheatsheets often lead pinners and other online visitors to a landing page. Landing pages typically contain email signup forms that ask viewers for their email address in exchange for something of value, like an offer you make that might involve a lead magnet item such as a workbook or free ebook. There are thousands of free offers on Pinterest that are considered lead magnets because they lead people to a landing page and request and email address in exchange.

The Case for Landing Pages Instead of Home Pages or Product Pages

Why would you create special pages, and multiples of them, just for people to fill out a sign up form? Why not just use your home page or product page? Great questions.

Home pages are for anyone and everyone, and not written specifically with a certain customer in mind. That's the beauty of landing pages and everything they offer—you can tailor the language and customize the images, and not have them listed anywhere on your site, so you can quietly, behind the scenes, test things out for yourself. Home pages convert no one. They are a generic front for your entire business. So, they convert no one in particular.

Sure, you may have a CTA above the fold on your home page, smack-dab in the center, but who is it really for? What happens if you start getting interest in a product intended and worded for college students, but you're getting a ton of traffic from 40-50 year olds with college degrees flooding to your website home page? You'll have a flood of bounces. That's why it's important to write for a specific person in mind on a landing page so you can cater that copy to one person.

So with that in mind, how many conversions do you get on home pages versus a purposely-crafted landing page? A lot less, I'd bet, and I've experienced the same outcomes time and time again. Almost all of my email sign up submissions happen on landing pages and not my home page. Landing pages convert much higher in comparison to home pages.

I know what you might be thinking. *This is a lot of work.* Hey, I know it is! I've done the work. But here's something positive to look forward to. The minute you commit to changing your mind about landing pages and put in the work required to build them, and launch them on Pinterest, you're going to give yourself a data goldmine.

You're going to be able to figure out why such-and-such product hasn't been converting well and what images work better, your sales will go up, and your email list will actually grow for once instead of gaining and losing a few subscribers every single month. And that's worth something big.

"My homepage has my three products on it. By sending traffic to my home page, I'm making them aware that I have these products for sale. Plus, I have all sorts of

testimonials and benefits of the products on there, too. THAT alone will transition them into being able to make a purchase decision. My home page is the ultimate landing page."

I see this argument a lot with marketers. They make a fair point. But, remember the **ultimate goal** is conversion. While you might be making visitors of all kinds aware of your products on your home page, they're still in the awareness phase, and there's no real call to action there. And you'd have to keep the copy pretty generic in order to appease everyone who might be going to that page. The focus needs to be on **conversion**. Not cold-turned-warm awareness with the hopes that they'll just buy based on the fact that there's a product there with testimonials and benefits.

And although readers and Pinterest users *are* "landing" on a home page, I'll say this again:

A home page is not a landing page.

Pinterest users will encounter hundreds of micro-moments where they're poised to make a purchase decision in a short amount of time, which is why you need to point them exactly where you want them to go.

Think of home pages as a gateway to the rest of your website. Home pages are for readers at **every stage** of awareness to what you offer. This makes writing the "perfect" home page copy a bit of a rollercoaster ride.

Landing pages are like fine-tuned conversion machines. They follow specific design and writing principles that have been shown to be more effective in transitioning readers into buyers time and time again. They'll help you squeeze every email address, opt-in and sale you get your hands on. *Trust this process. It works.*

Suppose you want to offer specific discounts or write custom messages to various demographics of readers. For example, existing writers who have published a book versus writers who haven't, the simplest way to communicate to that class of reader is by writing and creating separate landing pages, so you can speak to that one reader in mind. In this way, landing pages help you keep your message honed in on that one reader —private, personal, and not listed or done on your home page menu bar—without interfering with your general content on your home page.

Not all promotions are for all people.

Your homepage was never meant to be more than a central hub for a general audience. A starting point, if you will. Whereas landing pages have every single element designed, tested, and optimized for conversion. Optimized for the kind of customer you're trying to attract.

Home pages are static. There can only be one. But landing pages? You could have thousands if you wanted to, all written and designed for various products and types of customers.

One Reader, One Path

Every time you create a landing page with Pinterest in mind, I want you to keep in mind who that customer is. This is your Optimal Realistic Customer Avatar (ORCA) discussed in Copy Cocktail. Design each landing page with that ORCA in mind, and one idea or offer. Speak directly to that one person in mind, and talk to them as if you're their friend. One. Not a collective of people. So avoid using language like "all of you" or "you all", "everyone", or "hey friends". Speak to one person, and keep the offer to one thing.

No more, no less. Just one.

The purpose of the keeping this in mind is to encourage a conversion. It gives your reader a single path, and it's like you're speaking directly to them while they're at home on a Saturday night devouring a pint of ice cream in from of their favorite Netflix show, while trying to figure out various things in their life. You have a 50/50 chance of getting the conversion. What you do from there is completely up to you. *Hint—read Email Marketing Magic. It'll tell you what to do next.*

A landing page takes away distractions by removing navigation, links competing for your reader's attention, and alternative options so you get your reader's undivided attention on a single offer. Complete attention means you can lead your reader where you'd like them to go, i.e., to your sign up form. You're specifically designing for conversion from Pinterest or a form of ad or social media, even organic search.

The Argument in Favor of Segmentation

Knowledge is power in any form of marketing, but it's particularly true in search-based marketing efforts like on Pinterest. If you gain an understanding of what your readers respond positively to, you can make your pinning and general marketing efforts more effective.

Let's suppose everyone provides their email on the same landing page. Where did they come from? What marketing effort prompted them to convert?

If you have multiple landing pages with different offers or different variables, you'll get a clearer understanding of which offers on your landing pages work and which don't. Give yourself your own data! You put in all this work—why not benefit from data that your Pinterest account and website analytics gives you?

Creating multiple versions or even segmenting allows you to further segment your audience so you can market to them with more relevant offers, eliminate your weaker offers, and present your subscribers with targeted offers. You also have more information for updating your buyer personas.

In addition, the more landing pages you have, the more likely you will be noticed by search engines, especially if you've taken the time to work on your long-tail keywords and phrases. Be sure not to simply create multiple landing pages with the same copy. That is going to backfire for rank, and could even hurt your rank.

Promote your landing page by linking to it with your social media and other ads as well as your blog posts. Google will give your site credit if it has a lot of incoming links from external sources because it signals credibility and popularity.

Now that you understand the importance of using landing pages and why your home page just will not do it, let's cover landing page best practices to make sure your pages are set up properly to convert all that Pinterest traffic you're going to get.

Landing Page Best Practices

How protective are you of your personal data? How much data are you willing to give up to get something for free? What makes people hand that kind of data over to a complete stranger on the internet?

Never ask people for more than what you actually need. Email address and first name is perfectly acceptable.

Users are becoming less and less trusting of forms that request phone numbers. I remember signing up for something I really wanted—a case study if I recall correctly—and the form requested my phone number. In good faith, I submitted my information. All of a sudden, I had an email in my inbox asking when was a good time to call me about XYZ product (which I hadn't even been introduced to yet online) and then, shockingly, an hour later, I had a call coming in and a voicemail was left.

That experience left me with a really icky feeling. It actually felt invasive. I never wanted a phone call in the first place, or someone emailing me requesting my time on the phone. I thought I was only signing up for the case study report. And you certainly don't want Pinterest users getting an icky feeling about your brand by collecting more information than what you tell them they're getting. So don't ask for phone numbers, company names, unless there is an actual business need to do so, and they know you plan to interact with them on those levels outside of receiving your lead magnet promise.

The very best landing pages ask for minimal information and over-deliver on their promises. Bundled bonuses, surprise downloads, a welcome packet, or even exclusive access to media they weren't expecting are great ways to get your Pinterest user excited about your brand and wow them from the first interaction. *Just a hint when you're in creation mode.*

So let's go over other best practices, listed below for your learning benefit:

- Write a benefit-focused (not feature-focused) headline
- Design a unique image that shows the offer—a mockup, screen print, or the product in use
- Type up compelling copy that leads your reader down a path to the desired outcome of the landing page
- Position your sign up form above the fold (the part of the website before you have to scroll to see more) and

only ask for the data you actually need to deliver
your offer
- Write a clear call-to-action that stands out—you
want it to abundantly obvious what you want the
visitor to do
- Offer a lead magnet download, offer or a freebie
- Show value in why the download, offer or freebie is
valuable and worth their valuable time
- Remove any kind of navigation away from the page if
you're able using the theme or page designer you
have, including a menu bar
- Make sure your page is responsive, so that it loads
perfectly on all forms of devices (use a site like
ready.mobi or https://responsivedesignchecker.com)
- Be sure to use a plugin like Yoast to optimize your
landing page for organic search (great practice for
Pinterest keywords, as well)
- Create a thank you page to redirect the reader to
when they've submitted their information

Let's break it down and get into detail on what to do here so
that all that Pinterest traffic gets put to good use. Because a
pin lasts forever, and you don't want to make a critical mistake
in launching a landing page, possibly turning off thousands of
readers. You're going to nail this, I know. But just to be sure,
here are the details of each must-have in the list above.

1. WRITE A BENEFIT-FOCUSED HEADLINE, **not**

feature-focused headline. Granted, you're going to have people bounce off your pages for various reasons. In fact, the current statistic or average is that 70% of your visitors will bounce and say "see ya" without engaging with your content any further. Let's try to keep that number to a minimum, shall we? They need to know straight away what they're going to get and what's in it for them. The headline is the first impression. They *will* read the headline. Keep it concise, and clear.

Your headline needs to draw them in. Intrigue with a challenge or a wild benefit. Focus on the pains or gains (see Copy Cocktail for more on this and other customer psyche writing tips). Sadly, many people won't read your landing page copy, but they'll allow their eyes to skim the headline and subheaders. Maybe even some accent text. So take some time and really think about what kind of message you want that headline to convey. What's in it for the reader?

2. DESIGN **a unique image that shows the offer—a mockup, screen print, or the product in use.** Obviously, visuals help sell your offer, paid or not. So images are mandatory, and should reflect your target audience. What kind of tone or feeling should the reader feel? Does your image match that tone or feeling? How will your reader feel once they put your offer to use? (Please don't use cheesy stock photos of a man or woman in a suit cheering in the office. No one actually does that.) Certain images will work better than others, so this is an opportunity to test images as variables between various landing page copies.

. . .

3. TYPE **up compelling copy that leads your reader down a path to the desired outcome of the landing page.** Words matter! And clever copy rules. If you're not super awesome at writing copy, this is a skill worth learning. You certainly don't want to spend all that time writing the perfect headline and designing the perfect image and then completely bomb with your copy. Your copy will sell your call to action. It needs to be clear, concise and should lead your reader to the action you want them to take. As discussed in Copy Cocktail, compelling copy that speaks directly to the reader in using "you" and "your" helps to make them feel engaged with your writing voice.

4. POSITION **your sign up form above the fold (the part of the website before you have to scroll to see more) and only ask for the data you actually need to deliver your offer.** Your sign up form needs to be abundantly accessible and obvious in the event that your reader wants to convert right away. Don't make them search for your sign up form! "Above the fold" just means that readers don't have to scroll down or even to the bottom of the page to get to the form. The sign up form is in view as soon as the reader's device loads the page. This could be an embedded form or an anchor link to the form for ease of sign up. Here's a challenge for you: design your form to scroll with the reader as they move down the page. Holy smokes, Batman! You'd rock it.

You want to gather as much information as you need (not as much information as possible) about your reader. This largely depends on how well they know you, where they're at in the journey (this could be a landing page for people who are already prior customers), and how much they trust you. I only ask for name and email address. Ask for as little information as you need in your sign up form to create a low risk feeling to enter their information. A name and an email are sufficient to nurture a new lead generated from your landing page.

5. WRITE **a clear call-to-action that stands out—you want it to abundantly obvious what you want the visitor to do.** Call-to-action (CTA) items are probably the most important element on your landing page, although there are several elements that could lead to a conversion. The CTA button, message, or image needs to stand out. Meaning, you should use a color that contrasts with other elements on the page, but a color that still complements the look and feel. Some people resort to red because it's such a bright color and grabs attention. Don't do that.

Contrast can work well with any color—and it's the name of the game here. Suppose your brand colors are mostly turquoise… you'll want to choose a color like purple that can draw a reader's attention. There are plenty of colors you are probably using in your page palette or brand that could work for a CTA button or boxed area.

For the button or actionable element, this is not an area where you want to try to be clever. Be obvious and commanding in a sense about what you want readers to do. Action verbs work great. "Submit", "download", or "get it now" work incredibly well.

When it comes to the design of your CTA, there are a few tips and best practices that will make your action element so alluring that readers feel compelled to click. So just to review, your CTA includes the button or boxed area, as well as the copy you use to draw attention to it, in lieu of putting bright blinking lights around it like an airplane landing field.

Here are some additional best practices geared for CTAs:

- Design your CTA area with a vibrant and contrasting color that is branded and matches the overall tone and feeling of your landing page
- Focus your CTA copy on the benefits your offer has for your reader
- Five words or less on the CTA keeps things succinct and to the point
- The button or boxed area needs to stand out on the page—make it fairly large
- Breathing room is essential—give it some white space and don't crowd the area with other actionable things
- Use arrows that point to your sign up form or CTA button (completely optional)
- Insert anchor text that brings readers back to the form when clicked (super helpful)
- Check the overall flow of the page and place your

CTAs in areas where the eyes naturally go—typically to the right or below the text copy

- Test your button shape and color, as well as your CTA copy specifically

With all of this put together, I know you're going to rock the house with your CTAs. Definitely add this area as a testing mechanism or variable when you're creating copy versions of your landing pages.

6. OFFER A LEAD MAGNET DOWNLOAD, **offer or a freebie.** When you're using a landing page format as a lead magnet page to get leads and prospective new customers, you need to think of that page as part of your reader's journey or path to your ultimate offer. Your ultimate offer could be a low-risk, low-cost item, leading up to a higher-cost product or service, or your biggest product/service you offer. Your landing page for your lead magnet includes your initial offer—the item you give in exchange for your reader's email address. The item itself has to be compelling enough for your reader to provide their info, but it should also be relevant to your product or service you plan to introduce them to. (See Email Marketing Magic for detailed information on how to do this).

Let's say you sell pencils. I love pencils. Your offer might go something like this: "Mega List of 50 Different Types of Pencils, by Function and Purpose, to Draw Your Best Art". Ultimately, you're going to ask your reader to buy your pencils down the road. But notice that your lead magnet offer on your landing page is a list they can download. Not a report on graphite mining or pens, which you do NOT sell. That would be weird and not support your upcoming messages. You want to have excellent alignment between your initial offer and your products/services.

7. SHOW VALUE **in why the download, offer or freebie is valuable and worth their valuable time.** There is a sea of free downloads and, likely, similar products to yours offered on all sorts of websites. Why is this particular freebie or offer different than others? What makes this offer stand out from the rest? What are the benefits? Be sure you're not offering an "empty" freebie—one that lacks value or real purpose. Skimpy checklists are not the way to go here, chief. There's already and abundance of those on the web.

8. REMOVE **any kind of navigation away from the page if you're able using the theme or page designer you have, including a menu bar.** When designing a landing page, the mission is simple. Only give them the option to convert. Not to go anywhere else. Any other sort of link or distraction will keep the reader from entering their info and converting. So you have to remove as much as you can—like menu bars, sidebars, panels, and other items that could be competing for their attention.

. . .

9. MAKE **sure your page is responsive, so that it loads perfectly on all forms of devices (use a site like ready.mobi or https://responsivedesignchecker.com).** You'll want to make sure that your landing page displays well on every device. So it needs to be responsive, in that the sizing needs to meld for the interface being used by the reader. Using those two resource links will help make sure your page loads great in just about every device possible. So that no matter what they're viewing on, they have an equal opportunity to convert.

10. **Write to be discovered. Organic search is critical. Be sure to use a plugin like Yoast to optimize your landing page for organic search (great practice for Pinterest keywords, as well).** So yes, you're going to be driving traffic to your landing page using Pinterest (which makes you a genius, by the way), and you can also use the landing page for email marketing, social media, online magazines, ebook supplementary material, and more. Your page should also be optimized with target keywords for your campaigns and organic search. Do this so that when someone searches for your preferred long-tail keyword phrase, they'll find your landing page. And, when you target a leads with a long-tail keyword or phrase with paid ads, those words should exist on your landing page, too.

11. **Create a thank you page to redirect the reader to when they've submitted their information.** Thank you pages can

do one of two things: 1) simply thank the reader for submitting their information and to let them know what to expect next or 2) thank your reader and offer them a tripwire product, that is only available to them at that point in time. You *could* just show a thank you message on the same page or abandon the idea of creating a thank you page altogether, but there are several reasons why that's probably not a great idea.

Thank you pages are actually designed to 1) deliver the offer you promised on the landing page 2) give your reader an opportunity to see other relevant products they might be interested in 3) thank them (obviously!) for their interest in your landing page's offer 4) help you communicate what to expect next, and how you'll communicate with them in the future. All of these things go a long way in promoting yourself and committing to your brand promise to this reader down the road.

Now that you know how to craft the perfect landing page, you can design the perfect Pinterest images to support your landing page. In addition, you can take your existing landing page format, and try creating versions of it to see if other kinds of copy will work for you. This is a great opportunity to try out your various voices: humor, professional, succinct, modern, snappy, long-form, and more. For each landing page you create, you're going to want to follow the content modifier method and make around 60 Pinterest images to support your marketing efforts and drive traffic to your landing pages.

Designing Your Landing Page

Most of the time, design means layout, branding, creativity, colors, and gorgeous, meaningful pictures. In our quest together of crafting the perfect landing page for your website, we have to dig deeper than that. We're going to involve the principles of function, direction, and effectiveness into our use of the word "design". Get both left and right brain on board with this because we're getting crafty yet functional!

Landing Page Structure

You're in luck. Landing pages follow a pretty standard structure so you're not going to be starting from a hunk of clay here. They've been proven to work, so why try to create a new wheel? You can add your own flair for design and personality in your landing pages, and of course, add your branded elements and custom images. But trust me on this, stick to the standard format of thousands of converting landing pages and you'll be aces, chief.

So you already have the best practices earlier in the chapter, which you should follow to the letter in structuring your landing page.

Can your landing page include more than what the best practices require? Absolutely. You could add social share buttons. Pictures next to the people who have written testimonials. Quotes about what your offer has done for people. Charts. Graphs. Screenshots. Pictures of your dog.

Whatever you feel is going to help close the deal on that

particular landing page. The best practices list is simply the bare minimum and what I typically follow when I'm crafting these for my Pinterest audience. I've learned that sometimes keeping things simple is better. It really depends on what the pitch is.

You need to know you enough details about the ideal customer you're trying to attract, where they are coming from (in your case, they're going to be coming in droves from Pinterest) and that they're probably new to your landing page (most often the case—if it's a landing page geared towards repeat customers, then you'd word things differently, of course). The basic rule I recommend following is to include as much information the reader would need to convert. *Maybe skip the picture of your dog. Or be a rebel.*

Put on Your Spacial Abilities Hat

You're going to do a "looks good" test on your landing page. That means a few things… so here's a quick list of things to do before you hit that publish page and test everything out.

- Display the most important key info above the fold so they don't need to scroll to find it
- Do a blink test on your page—when you refresh your eyes on the page, you should be able to get the main message in less time than it takes to blink (or use the five second rule
- White space or negative space is your friend—it'll keep your visitor engaged and focused,
- Try to write with bullet points, checkmarks, or dashes

with short paragraphs to make your copy easy to read and comprehend

- F-pattern presentation works better than centered or justified. That's just how people scan pages of content online. Drive home key points in spaces and patterns that allow the eyes to naturally flow to that information

- Colors should be branded to drive your message home and adhere to your brand promise, which involves consistency

- Your unique style is more important than copying what everyone else is doing—be refreshing and express your unique brand—the more your Pinterest reader knows you, the easier it is for them to come to trust you

- Your top image sets the tone for the rest of the page —create a mood board for your landing pages, and you can reuse these images on your Pinterest pins, as well—a truly cohesive, branded appearance!

- When looking on your landing page, does it attract the kind of person you're trying to appeal to? Put yourself in that person's shoes—it's easy to get wrapped up into design and miss the bigger picture when you look at your landing page with fresh, objective eyes

- Does your landing page give visual cues of what to look at next? Do your images support your reader in signing up for your offer? Do the images reinforce your overall message?

- Check mobile device layout using the links provided
  in the landing page must-have list—your reader
  should be able to signup on the first screen they see

How does the page look? Crowded? Balanced? Informative? Fun? Use your spacial abilities and decide whether someone would be impressed with your page or if it looks like something from the mid-90's.

If you need more help or a template to lay your foundation, know I have Elementor templates in the shop to fix the whole scariness thing about designing a landing page. Elementor is a plugin for WordPress you can use on self-hosted websites to make designing landing pages super easy.

And when you're creating duplicates or copies of your landing pages for Pinterest traffic testing, it's nice to have that saved template feature so you don't have to design it all over again. Or, you can create a similar effect with the block editor on WordPress, but for landing pages, using the free Elementor tool is really helpful. Simply fill out your own information and points, add your own images, and voila, you're done in an hour. Visit shop.kerrielegend.com and go the Website Design & Logos section.

Landing Page Copywriting Tips

Stuck with what to say? Ah, chief, let's make this easy on you. You've come all this way to blow it on copy! Your primary objective in writing copy for landing pages is to be compelling, instructive, likable, concise, effective, trustworthy and informative all at once. No pressure, right? Like I said, let's keep this easy.

(Hint—reading Copy Cocktail from front to back will help you out on this and speed up your writing process. Just saying.)

1. COVER THE MAIN POINTS. What is this thing? How does it work? Why should your reader buy it? What are your ideal customer's pain points? What's frustrating them? What's keeping them up at night? What's keeping them from getting success like you've had? Pose those points or questions on your landing page. How does your solution work? ***Show the features.*** How does your solution improve their current situation (or one they'll have in the future if they stay down the same path they're on)? ***Show the benefits.*** How will they know your offer works? ***Show the social proof.***

How can you help that one reader you have in mind? What you don't want to have are listed points on why people think you're awesome or what makes you qualified. What matters to them is the offer—the product—and how THAT is going to make their life better. It's not about you. It's about them and whether that product or offer is going to be a good match. Your awesomeness is already implied by the quality of your website and your ability to launch this product, along with all the time and effort you put into it.

Pain Points

Pain points are the types of things that are barriers for your readers. They're also things that you can pin about on Pinterest as headlines. Remember our blog post about cheer in chapter 1? "Not enough cheer in your house?" "Is your holiday lacking in spirit and cheer?" "Want more cheerful kids?" Yeah— sometimes you have to touch on those pain points to get the reader's attention. And when they're coming to your landing page from Pinterest from a pin you created, those pain points probably have already been tapped, so in that case, you've already warmed your reader up to what they can expect.

Show empathy. Know and understand what they're going through. Tell a quick story. Have a solution in mind, and that is going to be your initial offer, with something you sell being offered after that. Empathy and communicating that understanding is an effective way to build trust. If they know you get their pain and struggles, then they're more likely to trust your solution. They want to relate to you. And being relatable is one of the biggest challenges people have in writing. So many writers get stiff with their word choice and need to loosen up and be themselves. I hope that's not you… *(ahem—see Copy Cocktail).*

Your Unique Solution

Draw them a path between their pain point and what your solution is. The path is clear. "Banish Grinchiness completely with this list of 10 ways to bring more cheer into your home!" "No more Grinch-filled holidays for you, chief!" "Download this list now and send the Grinch packing up the mountain!" "Melt the Grinch-y hearts with this list of cheermeister festivities!" The solution is just a click away in exchange for their email address or some green in their wallet. All their pains could go away with your solution. Time. Money. Unhappiness. You could be their next joy-filled discovery. Regardless if they had to shell out some sand dollars for it or not. If you become their problem-solver, more power to you and kudos!

Features

Features are the quantifiable elements of any product. They set the stage so the reader knows what's included. "500 templates. 1 Landing Page template. 50 Images." For ebooks, you may want to include a table of contents. Show the cover. If it's a webinar, indicate if workbooks or presentation handouts are included, along with how long you're going to tie them up. If it's a service, explain the process and what they get in exchange for their investment. Give them the stats. The data. The ingredients of your offer. They need to know this otherwise they'll come to you asking for buttered toast and jam to go along with their ebook download, so you need to set the scope of that offer.

Benefits

Load your copy with benefits because that's what your reader ultimately cares about. What's in it for them? Why should they bother with your solution? Features are cool and all, but benefits tell your reader how their situation will improve after using your offer. Paint them a picture of what your reader's life will be like after they use your offer.

Social Proof

It's persuasive. From logos of brands you've worked with to testimonials buyers have written for you and reviews of your product/services, studies have shown that social proof is effective to compel readers to take action. *They just want to know if it's worth it—their time and money—and if it works.* Have other people been satisfied? Are there raving fans who love it and are screaming their praises from their virtual rooftops? Provide social proof on your landing page, and you'll validate your offer without having to say another word.

All of these points combined in your copy will help communicate a compelling offer and start the process of removing doubts. But what if your reader is already approaching your page with objections? *"I will not spend money. I will not spend money. This person is probably like everyone else, they're asking too much money for whatever this is, and my problem will not go away. I'll end up wasting money."* Yeah. Let's talk about that.

2. GET AHEAD OF OBJECTIONS. Time to dismantle objections and be one step ahead of your reader. You have to help your reader, in writing, overcome the negative thoughts they've already developed about your offer. Let's get persuasive, shall we?

So you have your main points already written. Now you have to put on the shoes of your reader and think about everything they might protest.

"The lady doth protest too much, methinks"

- Hamlet, Shakespeare

For example, if you've stated that you've brought cheer to 10,000 happy households, better back that up with proof of your download count. Or show that you have some testimonials like "This brought so much joy to our holiday season! Thanks!" or "THE best cheermeister collection of tips ever!" Don't let your reader scoff at any of your claims. Back it up. Previews work as well, as do snippets or free trials, if they're applicable to your offer.

You're going to want to do this with every section of your landing page. If you're struggling with this exercise, enlist the help of beta readers or beta users. People that get a free copy in exchange for an honest review. Let them help you raise awareness to any objections a reader might have. I prefer to use objective people and not friends for this exercise because friends tend not to give you the unbiased answers you need.

So offer something up publicly over social media or use Pinterest to get a beta team together to test your products and offers out. You can then tighten up your copy, sharpen it up so you can get in front of objections and answer potential questions in advance, and use the feedback to learn and apply that newfound knowledge to other landing pages you create in the future.

. . .

3. GROW TRUST with your reader. "This might work for you!" *Hmmm… might?* "This has been downloaded 10,000 times!" *That doesn't mean it's good.* I use a different test when I'm writing sales pages, and it's something you'll want to try. Communicate like you're talking to your best friend, who cannot find anything to be happy about over the holiday season due to a few deaths in the family. Would you be able to look them in the face and get real and be confident that what you offer actually helps? What would you say to them? *"Helping families build and spread cheer at every possible moment is my passion and what I excel in. If you give this list a try, you're going to find joy. And if you want the full guide to a cheer-filled life that I offer for $7, I know you'll have daily cheer and a happier life, like so many of my customers have had. Check out some of their feedback!"* Alright, now we're getting somewhere. Your overall goal is to be authentic, real, authoritative, and built trust with your reader.

Some other ways aside from social proof are to:

- Use your talking voice—not the proper voice that gets between your thoughts and the ink—so that you speak to your reader like you would person in front of you
- Provide stats that support and enhance your message
- Draw in case studies that are closely related to your ideal customer you've written your landing page for
- Be relatable. The vulnerable side of you that has your

human failures, bad experiences, mistakes, and whoopsie moments are honest. Honesty is powerful in writing.

Share what is relevant. Write what you think may give your reader insight and a leg up. Feed them bits and pieces along the way, leading them to your product or service. There's nothing wrong with asking to be compensated for your hard work if it helps your reader and is quality material.

4. USE CLICK ENHANCERS. These are designed to cast away any remaining doubt before a reader converts. They're bits of copy placed next or near to your CTA that nudges your reader over the edge of doubt and eases their mind.

Here are some click enhancers you can use to nudge your reader and provide a low-risk conversion:

- Money-back guarantee
- No-hassle unsubscribe—don't love me? No problem!
- Testimonial quote from a super happy customer
- What to expect paragraph or a short blurb
- Price slashed today only
- Privacy policy—because I respect you!
- or… another creative way you might think of!

Whatever you choose, click enhancers will give your landing pages the conversion boost they sometimes need depending on the type of person viewing it.

Now that you know what to include on a landing page, let's talk about all the different types of landing pages you can create for all this Pinterest traffic you're going to have coming in.

Types of Landing Pages

The beautiful thing about Pinterest is you can have an abundance of landing pages and multiple types of landing pages to promote yourself. *That's why I love it so much.* With social media you're limited to 3-4 posts a day otherwise you can slapped with "spam" activity. With Pinterest, as long as you're uploading pins of different URLs and consistently pinning pins from other bloggers accounts as well, you're aces.

You get to pick and choose which ones you want to use here. I think a healthy blend of at least half of them would get you on the ground running.

- Paid Advertising Landing Page
- Lead Capture Page
- Product Pricing Landing Page
- Squeeze Page
- Splash Page
- Click-Through Landing Page
- "Get Started" Landing Page
- "Unsubscribe" Landing Page
- Long-form Sales Landing Page
- 404 Landing Page

- "About Us" Landing Page
- "Coming Soon" Page
- "Thank You" Landing Page

1. PAID ADVERTISING LANDING PAGE. One of the biggest mistakes marketers make, even on Pinterest, is sending traffic to a landing page either through a post ad or a pin on Pinterest to a page that doesn't do anything. It's just a page of information with a product on it. A cold sell. Or just a blog post littered with affiliate links. Sending readers to the wrong type of page, landing page or not, is a complete waste of money. With this method, you're going to warm up your Pinterest traffic with a landing page first by collecting their information and giving them something for it. If you're going to spend money on ads, whether it's on Pinterest or anywhere else, make sure you're collecting email addresses and leading your reader down a path. You want *leads* from paid ad marketing. Not sales. Sales should be the secondary focus. Not the primary for paid ad landing pages.

Paid advertising landing pages should do one thing: collect email addresses. Ask for one thing (or a name too if you want). The email address.

I always encourage my readers to master one thing first. Anytime you learn something new Then work on the next thing. Become intensely interested in the one goal and master it before you move on to anything else. This would be one of those times. *Get the email address.*

2. LEAD CAPTURE PAGE. A capture page is similar to a squeeze page, which you learn about in this chapter. These typically capture more information than just an email address. This kind of landing page is more relevant for service professionals who charge a high amount for their time who may need to weed out potential leads. Data like phone number, company name, number of employees, annual income, industry, role in the company, etc. are typically found on lead capture pages.

What are the goals you have in gaining data from the page? That should dictate what you ask for. In weeding out your leads and introducing your collected leads to your emails for marketing purposes, what do you actually need to know?

If they're at the top of the funnel, don't start with collecting 10 lines of data. Start with a name and an email address. If there's further interaction with your email marketing campaigns, then you'll want to send a landing page to collect more detailed information. There should be a demonstrated interest in what you have to offer before you start collecting more data.

3. PRODUCT PRICING LANDING PAGE. Suppose you have a new product or service or you're releasing new pricing or tiers. You could use a product pricing landing page to show

the reader their options in some of your packages or services. This is one page that should be optimized heavily with keyword phrases so that you can be found easily organically.

What's great about the product pricing page is you can leave an option open, too, in case you have a reader with special pricing needs. Boxes like "Need custom pricing or more options?" are often found on these kinds of pages so that you don't completely rule out other opportunities in working with customers.

4. SQUEEZE PAGE. Email marketing remains in the top spot for most effective means of conversion *(hint-not landing pages—those are just part of the starting point!)*. So squeeze pages play a vital role in getting a reader started in an email marketing sales funnel.

The goal of a squeeze page is to get the reader's email address. Nothing more. Once you capture the email address, you can start a trigger to nurture the reader with email marketing offers and other relevant content pertinent to their learning phase about what you do and what you offer. Plus, you can send them surprise downloads and freebies along the way, building on your brand promise and establish further trust.

You can use gated content or a single field prompt to have the reader enter their email address to receive a workbook, ebook, case study, checklist, cheatsheet, list of resources, a gated how-to article for members only, newsletter, whitepaper, or other content offer.

Squeeze pages are supposed to be super simple. Don't make these complicated. In fact, some of the best ones just have a banner with a field and entirely tempting headline. Just be sure to make it easy for the user to click out of the page if they're not interested or provide some element of confirmation that the form data was submitted successfully.

Some bloggers, I've recently noticed, are "forcing" people to enter in their email address to make a semi-transparent bottom or side banner go away. Entering your email address is the only way to make it disappear. Otherwise, it covers the material on the blog post you're trying to read. Some bloggers must think this is effective and a surefire way to get subscribers.

It's not. It's entirely annoying and a good way to repel readers from reading your material ever again. So don't use something like that. Keep it real and authentic and use a special page. Not a pop up banner or overlay piece that hides your content.

Pinterest pinners are savvy people and don't liked to be tricked into signing up on forms. They'll block your account in a heartbeat if you toy with them.

5. SPLASH PAGE. Splash pages are typically used when a reader clicks on a social media like or a content link. Instead of going straight to the piece of content, there's a splash page that acts as a buffer before the content is displayed.

Splash pages might hold important announcements, present

an ad to the reader, highlight something new, or even attempt to collect an email address prior to delivering the content. They might even collect minor data like age, demographic, a yes/no question, preferences, etc.

6. CLICK-THROUGH LANDING PAGE. In Pinterest Marketing I tell my readers to plan to give, give, give. You have to give value before you ask your readers to be compensated for your work product. Click-through landing pages help with that in that they provide an element of value before tapping on your reader's wallet with a request for payment. No reader wants to be hit with a "Buy Now" button when they're first getting to know you.

This is the kind of landing page that shares features and benefits, with a quick CTA button that encourages your reader to get a freebie of sorts. Once they click on that button, they're often taken to another landing page, typically a tripwire offer, which provides pricing details for related products and services, or requires payment information to begin a trial or to get the full version of something you offer.

What has happened by the second landing page is that the reader is primed and already educated on why they should take action and move towards a paid product or service. Then, typically a payment landing page emerges or a checkout page appears, and the reader then becomes a customer. This is where you can start documenting page abandons and determine if the information on the initial pages is enough or if your pricing is on par with current market, and make some decisions from there for tweaking and editing.

7. "GET STARTED" Landing Page. A "Get Started" landing page often is found above the fold that briefly explains the benefits and how easy it is to get started with something you offer.

There's typically a "get started" button on the page, begging to be clicked. It's the only button on the page. Ah, but don't forget to include a text link that has "Need more convincing?" and a page to take them to if they need ore information to make an informed decision. From there, you can take them to a series of FAQs or additional, detailed information.

8. "UNSUBSCRIBE" Landing Page. Unsubscribes happen even to the best bloggers. Sometimes a reader will decide that you're not their cup of tea. Maybe it's the way you write or the language you use. Maybe what they thought they would receive didn't match up with their needs. Make sure you have a way for your reader to unsubscribe and thank them for their time. Give them a change to manage their preferences or adjust the content they receive. Offer one last attempt or offer to keep them on your list. Like a "before you go" type of offer. Let them know you'll still be around if they change their mind and want to "get back on track" with what you offer as a solution. You could also include various links to your website

that they might not know about as a last attempt to regain them as a reader.

Just because a reader doesn't want your emails sitting in their inbox doesn't mean that they don't enjoy reading your material. They may still browse around. So a second chance button can prompt the reader to re-subscribe, just in case they were initially turned off by something or they realize just how talented and cool you really are.

9. LONG-FORM SALES LANDING PAGE. No joke, long-form sales landing pages take a while to put together. Succinctness is not your friend. You have to think of every possible question your reader might ask about your offer or product/service, every barrier or risk factor to purchase they may have, and list out every benefit you can think of so that you can assure their proper enjoyment of your product/service.

These work great with a video that tells the reader all about your offer. Why is now the right time for them to take advantage of the offer? Who has already benefited from the offer / product / service that would be of interest to a Pinterest user? This is where you can add names and pictures of people who write testimonials and have successfully used your offer.

You could also include some quotes, links to join your email list, read other testimonials, discover other products and services you offer, and end with a CTA button to take more action. You might even consider a sense of urgency or a scarcity element. We'll talk more about these soon.

This is not at all a minimalist approach, but one that deserves attention and length. You're going to experience some readers that need a lot of information before making a decision to sign up for something or buy from you. You'll need a lot of detail. But just like writing long-form blog posts, you can gleam a lot of insight and useful content for your Pinterest pins by going through this exercise. The goal of this kind of page? *To close business.*

10. 404 Landing Page. Whoops! You've landed on a page that is no longer in service. *But why?!* Hey, it happens. A mistyped link that can't be undone or modified on hundreds of Pinterest boards, a deleted post or page by accident, etc. 404s are never fun, but at least you can have fun *with* them, by redirecting your reader to something else or to offer to get them back on track. Hey, I've even used them as an opportunity to get an email signup in the process. Get creative and human with this unfortunate experience! Get them back to your most popular landing page as soon as possible or what would be considered as a neutral landing page.

Gosh, you could even direct Pinterest traffic here on purpose, if you get clever enough. You could offer three options: go to the blog, get a freebie download for their trouble, or offer up a free tutorial or "hi there!" custom video.

11. "ABOUT US" Landing Page. A lot of bloggers do about

pages all wrong. It's not a page just to focus on you. You can use it to get sign ups, as well. You can add wisdom, humor, your mission, list of passion projects, an invitation to join you on your journey, a link to your shop so people can get familiar with your work, add your social media links, or even just offer a lead magnet for visiting your about page. Answer the question: how can I move forward with you? An "I love your work—what do I do next?" works beautifully for a page like this.

12. "COMING SOON" Page. A coming soon page can act like a pre-order in a way. Get sign ups to send out an email about the launch on the date of with all of the product details included. They'll then get a final launch email when you're finally ready to reveal your new, exciting offer. Don't leave your landing pages incomplete. Use a coming soon page with a sign up form to get the release information instead.

Give them a teaser, put a launch date or anticipated launch date, and a CTA that asks for their email address so they can get notified when everything goes live at once.

13. "THANK YOU" Landing Page. Most thank you pages are a bit too succinct with a simple thank you. They could do so much more! Put it to work. You could include additional offers and gifts, free advice that leads them to see of your best pillar content, or whatever you think would be a unique angle for you.

The thank you page has traffic on it with a reader who is already excited to learn more. So don't waste that opportunity and take advantage of their highly motivated state of mind. You can also use it as an opportunity to collect more refined data about your reader, so that you can cater to their needs more completely.

How to Choose the Right Landing Page for Your Campaign

Now that you know about the most common types of landing pages that successful Pinterest Business user like yourself should use, best practices and how to design and write them, the next question is: How do you pick the right one? You don't. You try them all and see which ones work for you and bring traffic to them via Pinterest pins. Easy peasy.

This is really going to be an exercise in both design and writing for you. Do it once, and you'll be that much more equipped to launch another product now that you've had the knowledge and practice.

Begin by asking yourself these questions any time you're preparing a new landing page.

- *"What are the goals with this page?"*
- *"What are my competitors doing that I could do better on this page?"*
- *"What does my audience need or want to see to make a decision from this page?"*

- *"How did my audience get to this page? At what stage of awareness to my product or brand are they in?"*
- *"At a minimum, what do I want my audience to do when they leave this page?"*

Understanding the goal of the page needs to be made before you decide on what type you create. Answering these questions will guide you on the decision process of whether the page should be a short- or long-form landing page.

Short-form landing pages will include your "thank you", "unsubscribe" and "squeeze" pages. They're just a short design and writing job with a little engagement ask of your reader. Only the squeeze page will be worthy of creating pins for in this sense.

Sales pages, click-through landing pages, and product pricing landing pages are more long-form. They require more of a bigger ask of your customer and with bigger asks, you need bigger landing pages. Hence, long-form.

So how would this look with Pinterest being the primary driver of traffic? Great question. Let's get to it.

All of your Pinterest traffic is going to assume that they're NEW people to you. So the landing pages you create will assume they're not familiar with your brand or your products yet. So you'll be writing in introduction mode and making the reader aware of your products and services, and your other offers.

Now, yes, you'll probably have people who are already aware of your brand or website coming to you from Pinterest. But maybe they haven't seen *this* page yet, especially if it's brand new.

Once the reader takes action and creates a trigger event, like an email sign up to one of your offers or products, you can then introduce landing pages to them that are more informed and tailored to the reader, based on what you already know they're interested in. That way you can continue selling to them and providing value. And you do that by creating value-add email campaigns that you can learn about in Email Marketing Magic.

At this point, I don't care about what my competitors are doing. I familiarize myself with what they're producing for product and services, but I have my own game going on. And you will, too.

You are now competing with yourself. You don't give a crap about who's making what and how much they're making or how many likes they get or how many comments. None of that matters. This is now a race against yourself. Only you will know the numbers. Only you will know how much money you're making and whether or not what you're doing is working. You are in complete control of a machine you're building. This is the beauty of the *self-challenge oriented part of Pinterest* that I love.

With each long-form landing page you create, you'll create 60 or so images and release them over time, but ensuring you get them out to your tribes using the technique I showed you in chapter 2.

Remember how Pinterest images are really an ad that doesn't act like an ad? With each landing page, you're launching 60 ads out into the world in one day that you didn't have to pay for. And you *won't* pay for it. You just can't do that with social media.

Let's go back to our example of the cheer headlines and our list of 10 ways to add more cheer to your life. So when a Pinterest user clicks on your Pinterest pin with a headline about wanting more cheer in their life, they're going to go to your landing page that you've carefully written and designed, and get an email signup. Pinterest will record an engagement of a click-through. Over time, engagement will start to add up, and your pin becomes "popular". It's only a matter of time before you build an insane email list of people already interested in cheer.

Making Your Landing Pages Awesome

Before you start testing and launching your landing pages, there are a few things you can do to make your landing pages awesome, boost their performance, and focus on your reader. Here are some conversion-minded tips to get your landing pages roaring with growth.

DECREASE YOUR PAGE LOAD TIME. Delays in loading

your page means approximately 7% fewer conversions and 11% fewer page views. A three-second page load time can result in losing nearly half of your potential customers, according to a study. Slow-loading pages are frustrating for your reader. So landing page load time is a metric to take seriously.

KEEP **the buyer's journey in mind.** Since you're driving traffic from Pinterest to your landing page, you should know that your are more than likely dealing with a new visitor. They're not ready to close cold on your product offers, generally, without being warmed up first, so this is why you want to have landing pages created to make them aware first and talk about your solution. Your copy and offer should reflect this if you want to convert. It's no different from contemplating the stage of the mindset of the reader for any other marketing materials. You have to **meet your readers where they are** at the mindset level they're in.

CREATE A SEAMLESS EXPERIENCE. No surprises should be present on your landing page. Consistency between your pin and landing page so that you're continuing that initial path they took to get there is key. Use the same wording, the same image or a variation of the image, and same tone. Avoid bait-and-switching by all means possible. There might be a time when you decide that a piece of your content is no longer going to be free, because you got too many freebie hoarders ruining your metrics. That's ok. Offer something else instead, or point them where they can go to devour more of your content or get the same thing for a small fee.

ADD SCARCITY TO YOUR OFFER. Limited quantities, downloads or vaulting the item in the future is a great way to add scarcity to offers. Fear of missing out is a powerful scarcity tactic. This is considered an emotional marketing tactic, capitalizing on the reader's fears or a sense of happiness at the end of a carrot. No one likes to miss out, lose their ability to make a choice, or have something sell out when they've saved it to their cart for later. make sure your reader knows your item is in high demand and that it's going away soon. Rotate your offers in and out using this strategy and only make them available at certain times of the year. You may want to play with this strategy to squeeze a lot of high traffic email signups in a short amount of time.

Readers often want things that are hard to get. It's representative of value and exclusivity. Just like this book—it's the only Pinterest marketing tool that talks about the 7 methods of amplification for Pinterest specifically and you got your hands on it. You're going to have an advantage that other non-readers will not.

You can show scarcity by showing quantities left, use a countdown timer, or even with your words with phrases like "ending soon", or "last chance", "going away soon", "expires December 23" and so on. Only do this is the scarcity is true and you're going to stick with it. While your offer is unavailable, offer a signup squeeze form for a "waiting list" of sorts.

USE VIDEO. The entertainment that video marketing has is effective for conversion and assists in ranking pages higher. Plus, videos on Pinterest have been ranking in the first place in search as of the date of publication. Video has been proven to increase conversion by up to 80 percent. But it has to be an effective video that gets your reader to the ultimate goal—the call to action.

A lot of bloggers shy away from video because they don't feel pretty, attractive, or have a hard time speaking on camera. That's totally ok. I actually do all of my videos showing my desktop screen and a presentation. That's what I'm personally comfortable with. But if you're still on the fence about using video, here are some key reasons you might want to reconsider making the effort.

Video:

- increases conversion rates by letting your readers know who you are and helps them get excited about your offer
- provides a more personal message and starts the connection with you personally as a blogger and brand
- is often times more engaging than an image, and gets

the reader in the habit of clicking around (and eventually converting)

- will keep your reader on your page longer than a page with no video on it
- helps your reader process information 60k times faster than text

Excited about how to make your landing pages even more amazing? Just because you may encounter a poor-performing landing page doesn't mean it has to stay that way! When you start getting your metrics together and test your pages with the Pinterest traffic, which you'll learn more about in this chapter, you can make ALL your pages better. *Don't settle for a poor-performing landing page!*

Now, it's time to put all this knowledge about landing pages and how you're going to use them for your Pinterest traffic to work.

Pinterest is a Giant Testing Zone

If you've learned anything about Pinterest from me in Pinterest Marketing, you'll understand when I say that Pinterest is a giant testing zone. It's the perfect platform to test a bunch of pin ads without having to spend a single dime. It's also the best way, in my opinion, to test out your landing pages.

Not only are you going to test your pins for engagement and click-throughs, but you're going to test your landing pages.

Now if you're sitting there, reading this and thinking… but I just want to create and write stuff… ok, well, then do that. But maybe you're leaving money on the table. Maybe you're wording things on your landing page that could be presented better and you'd have more success with your online shop with just a few tweaks.

Testing pins and landing pages is just part of the job. Instead of making comments all day on social media posts that get me nowhere with sales or my overall happiness, I get to challenge myself daily to tweaking landing pages and creating better products for my audience. That's how you learn, and that's the task that needs to be done.

And it's a project (your website) that will constantly evolve and change. For the better, I might add.

If you're not willing to see the job through to the end, what's the point? All you'd be doing is potentially wasting time creating pins and pages that may not be working as you thought. How will you know unless you test them and look at the numbers? Really see where you could be leaving money on the table. It's worth the effort.

See it through. *Do the work.* I know you can do this.

Let's talk about how to A/B test your landing pages, because really, with the number of landing pages you're about to create with Pinterest in mind (and you'll totally blow your website up with traffic, by the way, if you do all this) you're going to be doing A/B/C/D/E/F/G testing. But just to keep things simple, we'll use the standard A/B testing or "split testing" name.

A/B Testing Your Landing Page

You have your landing pages created.

You have your 60 pins or so for each landing page, using my methods, up on Pinterest.

You've submitted all your pins to the tribes. You're releasing new pins every day to your brand's primary board.

You have your sales funnels written to nurture your incoming subscribers.

You have traffic coming in. Things seem to be working. Some things *aren't* working as well.

What's working on your landing pages? What isn't? Which pins are driving the most traffic? Why? Is it your pins? Is it your landing page? How do you know if the copy you chose is working? Why is the conversion rate low on one landing page but high on another? What needs to change? Which colors are performing the best? What's the conversion rate to subscribe? How many sale conversions are streaming through? What image is working the best? Why is this one landing page not performing well? Is it just because it hasn't had a lot of traffic yet? Or if your CTA placement is right?

Your business is different from others, and your target audience is unique. So this is a challenge against yourself to make things work for *you*. Block all the noise out and focus on the situation in front of you. *It's fixable.* Let's go over in detail how to best A/B test your landing pages. Like anything, let's start with a good foundation and do this from the ground up.

What is A/B Testing?

With split testing or A/B testing, you're comparing two or more pages, subtly changing one variable between each one to determine which one performs better. is simply splitting your traffic to two (or more) variations of a page to see which performs better. Suppose you want to start small and just test two pages. It's actually a great way to get started with something like this. Because eventually, you're going to want to test multiple pages that are pitching the same product (because we're going to pin the heck out of those landing pages!). While you could do this A/B or split testing manually by launching one variation change at a time, it's far more efficient to use a software that allows you to split test and can track your results.

I use Elementor for my landing pages. There is a plugin you can install that allows for split testing right inside Elementor (https://wordpress.org/plugins/split-test-for-elementor/).

Science class time! What happens when you change two or more variables at once? You won't know which variable gave you the positive change. So this is why you only change one variable at a time, or change one variable per duplicate copy of your landing page. The champion landing page is the one you will keep. But because you are launching traffic from Pinterest, you certainly don't want to have a bunch of traffic going to deleted pages (hello, need for 404 landing page that converts).

Instead, once you know it's a loser page, keep tweaking and editing it so that it's different enough from your champion landing page (your original page). This will help your Google rank and bring in traffic from a winning page that was once a loser. Your champion page is going to go toe to toe with your challenger page, or the page you modified or duplicated and changed a variable on.

HOW TO SPLIT TEST. So small variable changes—one at a time. Don't change your headline and image at the same time. Choose one to change. *Only one.* This isn't something you can shortcut. Then, create 60 pins to for each landing page, posing the same questions, headlines, but different images that match whichever landing page is being changed, if you're changing the images. You want to give each landing page an equal opportunity to become the winner. Change up the variables until you reach a conversion rate you're happy with.

WHAT SHOULD YOU TEST? There's a lot of variables you can change. You can test virtually anything on your landing page. But while that's possible, you may want to limit your test to a few of the most impactful elements of your page, such as:

- Headline copy
- Image
- CTA copy
- CTA color
- Click enhancers
- Your sales copy on the page
- Price of your offer
- Terms of your offer
- Benefits
- Features
- Order of how the information is presented
- Landing page form length, position, and fields

Try making simple changes first or what your gut reaction or feeling is on what might not be working. Testing these variable elements are going to have the biggest impact on your conversion rates.

Landing Page Metrics

Time to measure! Besides getting sales, the ultimate metric to gauge whether your landing pages are working, there are other metrics you can use to give your results a numeric value. Watching the numbers will help you gauge those tweaks to your landing page and whatever edits you make.

I recommend using a spreadsheet to keep track of changes and how they impact your changes. It doesn't have to be anything super fancy, just a way to check things week by week or whatever frequency you choose. Once you start getting a good conversion rate that you're satisfied with, you can stop tracking and move on.

PAGE VISITS. How many visits are you getting on your landing page? The reason why I like Pinterest so much is that you're going to get traffic. So many bloggers don't focus enough attention on traffic and try to use social media posts—endless posts—and paid ads to sell, getting limited response and traffic. How will you know if your landing page is good if you don't have traffic? Pin quality (image, keywords, applicable boards, etc.) and quantity of pins determines your page traffic from Pinterest. The more visits, the more you increase your probability of conversions. That's why we'll focus on frequency in chapter 5. Watch your page traffic carefully and which pins are performing the best so you can make more pins like the ones that are winning.

TRAFFIC SOURCE. Even though you're using Pinterest as your primary source of traffic, you may want to try other channels to bring in traffic, as well. You can see which channels are working the best by going into your Google Analytics reports. Knowing where your traffic is coming from and what the reader does next (which analytics will tell you) will let you know where you should double down on your marketing resources.

. . .

SUBMISSION RATE. This is the rate at which readers complete your landing page sign up form and land on your thank you page. All the tweaks and edits you make to your landing page elements will make this number fluctuate. So be sure to do split testing so you know what is working.

CONTACTS. Sometimes people submit forms twice, or decide that they want to have you send them what you offer to a different email address. Contacts differs from submission rate because duplicate contacts are only counted once. This will make sure you're getting an accurate count for a better conversion rate determination.

HEAT MAPPING. I love heat maps! Heat mapping software and plugins tell you exactly where people are clicking. Heat maps are crazy helpful. They observe how readers interact with your page instead of just spitting out a number. It shows where people scroll, where they click, and how far down they go on your page. They can also tell you what they read and what images they attempted to click on.

BOUNCE RATE. Your bounce rate will tell you if readers are coming to your page and immediately leaving. If they are, then maybe your content isn't aligned well with your offer. Maybe it's not capturing their attention. Or maybe they're not sure what they're supposed to do when they get there. Make sure your page is a reflection of your pin design and fulfills the promise your pin indicates.

SIGN UP FORM ABANDONMENT. If your online signup form service allows for it, this is a metric that lets you know how many people began to fill out your form but ultimately didn't go through with the signup process. If it's high, then try adding some click enhancers or tightening up the copy on your form. Make it abundantly clear what you want the user to do.

BENCHMARKS. What are each metric's norms? This is the point where you need to evaluate what the standard is for your industry. Compare and contrast, and then work to improve your metrics to levels above the norms. So the question will be, "am I on par with what's expected from my industry?" You might even surpass those benchmarks if you work hard enough.

No matter what's happening with your landing pages, you can diagnose and heal your landing pages if you give your metrics some attention.

Conclusion

The key to all of this is to stay organized. Use the parent/child tier system within your website's page and post framework so it'll be easy for you to identify and fix what may or not require tweaking or editing. *There's no reason or excuse for why you can't have a landing page that converts well.*

As long as you're following the best practices we covered in this chapter, you'll be on your way to a high-performing landing page that brings in loads of Pinterest traffic. And if you need additional guidance, check out my Art of Blogging Masterclass, which focuses on the three core foundations of blogging that will have the most impact on your career as a blogger: web traffic (Pinterest Marketing Amplification), copywriting (Copy Cocktail), and email marketing (Email Marketing Magic).

5 FREQUENCY METHOD

THE NEXT METHOD we'll cover is the frequency method. Let me start off by saying that there is no magic number in place that you should be pinning per day, week or month. But I will tell you exactly what I've been pinning and why that makes sense for me and my brand. And then, you can decide how much you think you should be pinning based on how much you're actively writing and what you can ultimately commit to.

The main reason why increasing your pinning frequency works is because of a simple fact—the more you're present and pinning to the feed, the more likely your profile will be discovered by other pinners. As a result of increasing your pinning frequency, you'll notice that your follower count increases respectively. And, you'll have many more re-pins (assuming you're pinning great material) as a direct correlation to having "more" out there for other pinners to discover.

Here are the benefits, which were tested on six Pinterest accounts we run:

- Your followers will increase dramatically, in a faster manner
- You will have more re-pins
- You will have more data on which of your boards are the most interesting and popular among your followers
- The mushroom effect—what I noticed was as frequency increased, so did everything else, from the then left column on Pinterest Analytics to followers, re-pins, re-shares, and conversion—it all starts with frequency

So the goal is primarily to grow in followers and awareness of your account and brand, along with increasing your re-pins and overall growth.

This is a subject that gets me fired up and quite heated under the collar because there's so much bad information and ridiculous warnings out there by self-proclaimed Pinterest experts who have no business making these statements. It's no wonder people are stumped. They don't work for Pinterest. They have no knowledge of the algorithm code. Where do they get these magical numbers from? Are these people aliens? Who seriously came up with this regurgitated crap?!

I digress. Let's dig in.

Are You Pinning Enough?

Pinterest Business users often are not pinning *enough*. And I can see why from two angles: 1) they're being told that frequent pinning can harm their reach and 2) it requires actual work. They're getting bad information from various places—on Pinterest, no less!

For example, this quote from a "pin coach" website.

The **maximum pin frequency** should be about **25 pins per day**. Anything more than this would be overkill unless your brand has a ton of **content and Pinterest-ready images** at hand. Start pushing far beyond that with your pinning schedule and you can actually harm your reach.

This is absolutely absurd. This comes from an "expert" account with less than 358k monthly views. I pin over 300 pins per day and it helped amplify my reach. It didn't harm it whatsoever. 25 pins per day really gets you nowhere in terms of profile reach. Your growth WILL be slow if you put a max at 25 pins a day. So don't buy into this notion that there are maximum numbers.

PS—This is a prime example of bad coaching advice. Sit your butt down, pin coach.

Let's break this down by the hour. 300 pins over a 24 hour

period is about 12-13 pins per hour. That's about 1 pin every 5 minutes. I'm also using an authorized pinning scheduler who partners with Pinterest. So I'm good at 300 per day, and I have enough content to support pinning from my own domain at 60 pins per day to follow a basic 80/20 rule of 80% others' content and 20% of my own. It's an excellent balance.

Another example of receiving bad information and data is on Buffer's website who you would think would know better than to make recommendations about platforms they're not that familiar with. They haven't updated it since pre-Smart Feed era and **Buffer recommends starting at 5 pins per day, and working up to 15-20**. Buffer as a company (a scheduling app that you can use for Pinterest) has less than 13k followers and around 447k page views per month on Pinterest.

Oh good Lord. Sit down, Buffer. Stick to app development.

So who's right? No one. There's no magic number. What anyone giving advice should really do is provide examples of what they're doing and why that works, *and let you try it and make a determination yourself for your own account.* So do you see why there's so much confusion coming from business marketers wondering why they're not being followed, discovered, seen, or re-pinned? Bad information everywhere.

This is the danger in relying on information from non-Pinterest-pro users. You can spot the pros by **3 ways:** 1) fresh pinning content on their websites (check the blogs) with recent pins 2) 10+ million in monthly viewers and 3) indicator of sales (screenshots, analytics, etc.). I am not the only pro out there. There are others, but they are rare and few.

Just because a site has a lot of articles with information about Pinterest, a podcast or even provides professional services for businesses and brands *does not make them a qualified expert.* It may mean that they know enough to assist you, but to truly understand marketing on Pinterest, you need to look at their numbers and analytics. The proof you're looking for is in the numbers and the consistency of those stats.

There is No Magic Number—Bottom Line

So I'm telling you right now and I hope this gets drilled in—there is no magic number. If you follow these methods, you'll do wonderfully. I do recommend working your way up to 300 pins per day if you can manage it with your marketing time budget. I think you'll have massive success when you're pinning 60 or so pins a day from your domain. And if it has worked for the six accounts that we run, I know it'll work for you, as well.

All I can do is offer up the data from six accounts we run to show you that pinning more frequently is the way to go.

Growing with Other Bloggers' Content

While we've focused on increasing the number of pins you pin from your own domain to get all that wonderful website traffic streaming in, you're going to want to balance that with relevant content pinned by other bloggers, as well. Finding great content isn't hard when you have the right tools in place or know some of the shortcuts to pinning efficiently.

Never be afraid to pin your "competitors" pins as long as provide accurate, helpful information. I actually refrain from pinning content from other Pinterest course providers because a lot of what they're stating or claiming to be true isn't, and that's not helpful for my readers at all. But for my competitors that DO get the facts right and offer valuable insight, I'm more than happy to re-pin and share their content.

You should do the same. It's how this blogging community gets along and forms long-lasting relationships.

There's a trick to this process in getting all that work done. Here are your options in terms of efficiency, in preferential order:

- Pin from your tribes first using the "save to draft" button on the pins you want to share, as described in chapter 2 (because you're committed to your tribes first and foremost)
- Pin from your group boards
- Refresh some of your older pins with new images, or revive older content with updated images using these seven methods
- Manually pin from your feed—both from who you follow along with your general feed

You want content that first meets your obligations and forms /

fosters relationships with other bloggers (your tribes), content from your group board to support other collaborators who might not be on Tailwind (group boards), dig up your older posts that are craving some Pinterest love (older blog posts on your blog), and go a discovery hunt on your phone or laptop with some manual pinning just to see what new stuff is out there.

Hint—these activities are incredibly idea-stimulating. Pinning and being on Pinterest in general is going to lead to a lot of new ideas and will teach you things you might not have known before.

All of this supports your overall goal of being more present on Pinterest, getting your pin quota up, and it also helps you discover new content outside of your "norms".

Frequency & Follower Count—A Direct Relation

Honestly, during the testing phase between December 2018-February 2019, I was surprised at my findings at the direct correlation between pinning frequency and follower growth.

THE STATS. I was at about 4,000 followers, give or take, at the beginning of December. I had grown from about 100 to 4,000 between February 2017 and December 2018. So it had taken a good year and a ten months just to grow by 3,900 followers.

And I know that followers really isn't a metric worth focusing on, because it's not really a Pinterest focus, either. In fact, recently, it's a metric that they've somewhat hidden from other users unless you really dig for that information.

So if number of followers isn't a focus… how come it helps so much in terms of growing? I'm not at over 23,000 followers, having grown by 19,000 followers in just nine months. What impact was I really making on my Pinterest account and my blog that

REACH. When you get followers, you have an opportunity to get in their feed. This then allows them to pin your material. Which in turn, is seen by *their* audience, too. So, in effect, it's the mushroom. You explode. It's the reach factor and being active in the feed that I think made the difference, and people take notice and follow.

EFFECTS. I tried not pinning at times after my research period—and started doing that in May 2019. I noticed a drop in number of followers per day. I went from 80-120 new followers per day to around 40-60. I was still growing, but only on the merits of all the work I had been doing, and my original pins being looped.

So you could theoretically just sit around, not create any new content, and rely on your existing pins to be looped constantly, and still grow. *Well, that's news.* Something to think about if / when you have a big project and you need to take a break from blogging and pinning. You *can* take a break and get focused on a project and not blog for quite some time.

To do this, you could have 60 of your domain pins being scheduled and looped per day of your existing content and not have to do a single thing. I certainly did it just to see what would happen. Zero impact on sales, and nothing else other than my followers per day count when I wasn't pinning 300 or more pins a day.

Full disclosure, my account did go down to about 9.2 million monthly viewers in June 2019 when I took a break, which felt like a punch to the gut, but during the summer of 2019, I was busy taking care of my son in the hospital in an entirely different state while also trying to get this book written. Which means my reach wasn't as high during that time. I took a break. And it was worth it. So just know you don't have to keep up the pace of intense blogging forever. You can allow yourself a break once you get going with these methods and focus on other projects, too.

RESULTS. Between December 2018 and February 2019, I only tested and research my own account. After that, just to be sure it wasn't a fluke, I tested five other accounts, and on top of that, applied some of the same processes and theories to other accounts I was working with. The results were consistent between over 20 accounts. Pinning frequency increase profile views, re-pins, followers, and overall blog traffic.

Conclusion

Pinning frequency, from a growth perspective, matters a great deal. If you're looking to grow your follower base, pinning relevant content frequently and using an organized method is the way to go to achieve this.

I see a lot of Pinterest accounts with X-amount of followers being sold and groups and forums. This isn't a shortcut. It's a bad idea. You only want to grow with people who are actually interested in your account and the kind of pins you create and share. Anything else is irrelevant.

Work on your pinning frequency and see what it does for your account. I'm excited to see some big numbers coming from you, and want to hear about your amazing results.

6 PROMOTED METHOD

THE PROMOTED METHOD involves using paid advertising, a built-in option to each Pinterest Business account, to bring awareness to your brand and videos, drive consideration through traffic and installation of apps you might develop, and get you conversions through pin engagement and click-throughs and catalog sales.

What are Promoted Pins?

Promoted pins are pins that show up on your Pinterest feed based on what you have pinned previously or what you are searching for, and are paid for by the original pinner with a business account. Promoted pins will be labeled with a bar that might say "Promoted by" along with the profile who is promoting them. Wording may change with updates, so just look out for "Sponsored by", "Advertised by" or "Promoted by" or something similar so you know it's a paid, promoted pin. This identifier is typically included at the bottom of the pin where the name of the board and pinner's profiled are located. They blend in quite well with the rest of your feed, and you have to actually look with intent to see that it's a paid pin.

Promoted pins are only available to business accounts. Like I covered in Pinterest Marketing, you need to have a business account if you're doing any form of commerce on your website, including affiliate links. It's also the only way to gain access to promoted pins and running ad campaigns on Pinterest. You won't note any difference between your user experience between personal and business. In fact, you'll just have access to more tools.

Here are a few benefits you'll experience when you switch over to a business account, if you haven't already:

- You'll have the ability to change your business name and username
- Access to Pinterest Analytics, which will give you insight into what your audience is pinning and which pins and boards are the most popular
- Ability to claim other accounts like Instagram, YouTube, Etsy, etc.
- Rich pin status—the ability to have your pin description automatically load through rich pins is a definite benefit!
- It's free. Doesn't cost you a dime. Only running

Pinterest ads will cost you money… and even then, it won't be as much as any other ad campaign you might have run on social media

- Different terms. Pinterest states on their website that "If you're using Pinterest for business purposes or as part of how you make a living, you should sign up for a business account and agree to our Business Terms of Service."

If you're making ANY money off your website or profile, you need to have a business account. If you have access to Promoted Pins, a screen like this may appear when you visit ads.pinterest.com.

OR, your Pinterest home page might look like this, with the Ads dropdown menu in the top left corner.

If you do not currently have access to Pinterest promoted pins and you have a Pinterest business account, you can request access or submit a help ticket through the Pinterest.

THERE ARE a lot of marketers who are hesitant to launch pin campaigns on Pinterest. This is one kind of advertising that isn't going to suck the life out of your marketing budget. In fact, Pinterest Ads surpass Facebook Ads in terms of return on investment.

Don't be scared. But before you start diving into spending money on Pinterest, here are a few pointers to know, from me personally.

- Make sure your organic version of your pin is converting and getting sales first

- Test various kinds of campaigns using the same pin or same landing page (where applicable)
- Don't spend more than you can afford—Pinterest bills two times a month—one time at the beginning of the month and another halfway through.
- The shelf life of a promoted pin is about 90 days

This past year I did a lot of testing with ads across six different Pinterest accounts, and arrived at some conclusions and recommendations, which I'll share with you in this chapter. But first, let's go over some of the benefits of promoted pins and why or when you might want to use them.

Benefits of Promoted Pins

Promoted pins can help you gain a more qualified audience. You want to find more of your people, right? This is a good time to remember that while there are a ton of great people on Tailwind and on group boards, that isn't representative of *all* Pinterest users. So by promoting your pins, you are reaching exactly who you want to be reaching, both users of Tailwind tribes and other schedulers along with people who *aren't* using Tailwind, and are more of a consumer user on Pinterest.

Promoted pins amplify your content. Remarkable content gains that coveted top spot in the Pinterest feed. When you're hitting the top spot of the feed, your content gets shared and re-pinned and clicked on even more than before .

Promoted pins will boost your audience engagement and click-throughs to your website. The shelf life of a Promoted Pins is 90 days! That's a long time. If I were to do the same advertisement on Facebook, I'd have less conversion in terms of sales and less signups, and pay a lot more money. Promoting on Pinterest, provided that you've already tested the pin and know it's a strong, converting pin that is generating actual sales for you, will give you a pre-qualified audience based on the keywords you put in and the description of your pin. Think of it as boosting a post on Facebook only for a lot less money and much more return.

Types of Promoted Pin Campaigns

There are currently, as of the date of publication, six different types of Promoted Pins campaigns that you can choose from (as long as your business is based the US, CA, or the UK, Ireland, Austrailia, and New Zealand).

The six campaigns are as follows:

- Brand Awareness
- Video Views
- Traffic
- App Install

- Conversions
- Catalog Sales

Each type of Promoted Pin prioritizes and optimizes for different results that you might be looking for. Each type charges based on the events or actions tied to those desired results. So, the campaign type you choose matters, and dictates what you're paying for and how much.

Let's dive into the types of ad campaigns that are going to help you amplify your reach and boost sales on Pinterest.

Brand Awareness Campaigns

Brand awareness campaigns are a type of Build Awareness campaign that allow you to be seen by people on the most visible parts of Pinterest. They **help people discover your brand and products, through various ad formats.** Awareness campaigns focus on reach, showing your ad to as many people as possible who have made searches similar to your keyword or have pinned to similar boards. They do not focus on action. You can use these to get pinners familiar with your brand—and let them know you exist—and give you visibility. Becoming brand aware on Pinterest is just one of the many benefits you'll get out of pinning and advertising there. Once there's awareness, there's engagement. It's an incredible tool for brand recognition purposes, and they give you much larger visibility than other types of Promoted Pins for the same price.

You'll be charged per every 1,000 impressions, which can save you money. You're focusing more heavily on reach instead of clicks in this kind of campaign. Pinterest's awareness campaigns can be purchased directly from Pinterest or through the auction, where you bid for placement.

Video Views

Video has become a booming presence in 2019 on Pinterest, so much so that you'll find that video pins in general are landing at the top of search. Video gets more engagement. We're loving video on Pinterest. Video ads help you get more views on your video, which means they're clicking on the video (counts as engagement) and watching it. They can also click through to a page to view a video there, too. They are similar to promoting a pin for a traffic campaign, only designed for video-specific pin content. I've seen bid prices as low as $.03 per click on this kind of ad campaign type. I think this is a format of content that Pinterest will be pushing even more heavily in 2020 and beyond. It wouldn't surprise me if Pinterest made even more features to support video in general, almost turning it into a mini-YouTube type of platform for video. Maybe even a new creator studio module for video makes? Who knows! We'll see.

Traffic Campaigns

Traffic campaigns are a form of Drive Consideration ads designed to send traffic to your site. Start using these after a few of your pins have shown promise in terms of engagement and conversion (sale or lead generation). I personally do not take out ads on pins that haven't had a chance to take foot organically. I like to measure the pin's response to the audience first. But if you want to drive lead generation or sales, this is a good campaign type to choose.

This is the type of ad that targets users on Pinterest who are into researching, and make buying decisions. These are your known shoppers with a history of converting from Pinterest to a website. Pinterest is able to send interested, ready-to-buy pinners right to your site. That's a huge advantage over other types of campaigns.

This is a PPC (pay per click) or CPC (cost per click) type of ad campaign platform, so be prepared to spend a little more for this type of ad. But in the end, if your landing page is great and your product is awesome, plan for some incredible sales results like Joe and I have had with our own traffic campaigns.

Don't just go for the "good bid" level—shoot for the high bid to start off with. Pinterest will give your ad more performance out of the gate with a high bid. You can always adjust the bid down to a level you're more comfortable with when you start seeing success from that ad.

If you need further help with this, join in on my Pinterest Amplification course where you can learn more about promoted pins and traffic ads. You'll see me set them up in videos and explain why I make certain decisions about pin advertising.

App Install

Let's say you have an app that you're trying to get users to install. You can use promoted pins to help you drive installs of those apps. I don't have an app for users to install, so full disclosure, I haven't worked with any ads with this kind of campaign, but you can still get some great tips from the Pinterest creative best practices for ads article available on Pinterest.

Conversions

For conversions, you'll be adding a tag. To me, it seems like the equivalent of a Facebook pixel. Then, you're going to install a base code. You'll add the base code to any page where you want to track conversions. If you want to use retargeting, you would add this code to every page of your site to create audiences to retarget to later.

Then you'll add some event code, but you'll only add this code to pages where you want to track conversions. The base code has to run before the event code.

To be clear, a page visit happens when your site loads a page. So you should add the base code and PageVisit event code between the <head> and </head> tags on the pages where you want to track page visits. You might want to work with your site's theme coder to identify where this code needs to be added, so the event records correctly. This is fairly easy to do in the Editor section of WordPress Genesis themes. Correct placement ensures the code runs as soon as the page loads.

If an event is triggered when someone takes a specific action (like a button click or form submission), you should make sure the event code is placed so that it only runs as a result of the action, and not because someone loaded the page.

There are nine events you can track in Pinterest:

- Checkout
- AddToCart
- PageVisit
- Signup
- WatchVideo
- Lead
- Search
- ViewCategory
- Custom
- User-defined Event

Finally, you'll need to install the Pinterest Tag Helper Chrome extension. It helps you check that your Pinterest tag is properly set up and successfully passing back the correct and intended event data, as well as validating whether you are sending the correct enhanced match value on any given page of your website. In other words, you want to make sure that a WatchVideo event is matched with a user watching a video and not a signup for your email list.

Again, this is a bit more techie and you might want to consult with an experienced web developer to ensure you have everything set up correctly. Once you do it, you'll have amazing data rolling in, helping you make better decisions on your marketing and pinning plans on Pinterest.

Catalog Sales

You can connect your product catalog to create new Pins that can be found on Pinterest, and then organize the full range of your products on your Pinterest ad and account.

Your data source should be a URL that links to a tab-separated (.tsv), comma-separated (.csv), or extensible markup (.xml) file hosted on an external site with metadata formatted in English.

According to Pinterest, they recommend doing the following:

- **Update daily**. We ingest your data source once every 24 hours. Make your updated full data source available daily to keep your product details up-to-date. We don't support scheduling or on-demand ingestion.
- **Host your data source**. Host your own data source on an FTP/SFTP server or with an HTTP/HTTPS direct-download link. This needs to be accessible by a user-agent, and can't require IP or SSH key whitelisting. If you're using a direct download link, there can't be any extra navigation required for Pinterest to access the file. We don't provide data source hosting.
- **Max 5 million products**. We can process up to 5 million products per account. If your data source has more than 5 million products, we'll process the first 5 million rows.
- **One data source per business account**.

Setting Up a Pinterest Ad—Promoted Pins

Once you have a pin that is worth promoting (high-conversion for sales, re-pins, click-throughs, engagement, etc.), you'll want to start promoting the pin. You can do this by clicking into the pin on your brand's board and you'll arrive at something like this:

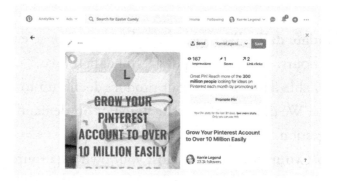

Click on "Promote Pin" and you'll come to a screen that looks like this:

Select your daily budget, make sure your link goes to the right destination, and your campaign duration. Select your target audience by adding keywords into the keyword box.

You'll be able to see the potential audience size and the total budget your daily spend will amount to.

The other way you can start promoting your pins is to go up to your top menu bar and click on "Ads" and then "Create ad". It'll look something like this:

Name Your Campaign and Choose Your Budget

Pick a unique campaign name that will help you remember what your goal is and which pin you're promoting. This will help you sort through your ads later and make modifications if necessary. Then, choose your daily or lifetime budget. This is the daily cap Pinterest will spend and also the total amount that the ad will cap out at for the duration of the ad.

Then, you'll be brought to the Ad Group Details page:

Enter the details that are specific to your pin. This will help you remember which specific pin you're promoting. I usually put the category name (my product) and then part of the headline on the pin design.

Targeting

Next, move on to targeting. You'll note that on this screen shot, I have several audiences. Over 50, actually, but you can't see them all from this screen. You can easily create audiences by uploading segments of your email list. You could also have an "Engagement Audience" which means a collection of people who have engaged with your pins in the past.

Select your audience and click on it below to "include" or "exclude". You can also use the search bar to find or create an audience.

You've got four options to create a new audience:

- Visitors who went to your site
- A list of customers that you upload
- An engagement audience that engaged with pins from your confirmed domain
- An actalike audience that behaves similarly to one you already have

Pinterest will then find people based on those actions or email addresses that you upload and match their accounts with your audience. Give it time; may take 24-48 hours to have the propagation work.

Then you'll have a list of audiences saved to your ad profile:

I would recommend setting your language to English, since my blog post is in English. You can adjust your gender preference as per the content of your post. You can also set to "All Locations" because you could have English-speaking individuals all over the world.

Add Your Interests

After you add your audience, you can select your interests with which categories your pin is most related to.

Keywords

Start by putting in your gut reaction long-tail keywords you

believe your audience would be searching for. Then, fill in the
gaps by using the "extend your reach" option on the right.

Take notice that your potential audience size will adjust and
fluctuate as you add more terms or change your keywords.
Click on the + sign to add recommendations and add those
keywords and phrases to your list on the left.

Demographics

Adjust Gender, Ages, Location, Languages, and Device
demographics to refine your reach.

Advanced Options

I typically use my ad group placement as "All". You might find a reason to use "Browse" vs. "Search". Completely up to you. You also have the ability to track the success of your ad by using the event type tracking. In a landing page scenario, you could put the thank you page after the user clicks on a signup to track how many conversions are coming through from your pin.

Budget & Scheduling

Decide how much you want to invest in the pin. You can set a daily budget and a lifetime one, as well. It'll help you set limits and not overspend.

Optimization and Delivery

The maximum CPC (cost per click) you're willing to spend is next to fill out. Pinterest gives you a suggested bid and lets you know what will be considered as competitive. Your bid rate is the maximum amount that Pinterest is going to charge you every time a pinner clicks on your pin as a result of it being promoted (your followers who re-pin it directly from your board will not cost you anything).

Select your pacing with how fast you want your pin ad to be displayed along with how fast you want your budget to be spent.

Experiment with your promoted pins. Try higher CPC with lower daily budget, lower CPC with higher daily budget, etc.

Select Your Pin

Find your pin design that you want to promote, or you have the option to upload a new image. You're not finally ready to promote your pin! Then, finally, you're ready to hit the launch button.

It will be in a pending status until it is approved, at which point your promotion begins.

What happens if your pin is not approved? If your pin isn't approved, you'll get an email from Pinterest. I've had promoted pins not get approved before. In some cases, it could be an issue with excessive hashtags, the value given to the reader or if the pin is solely promotional, readability, pin size, allowable content, etc.

Some final takeaways about promoting on Pinterest and my thoughts on when to pin: wait. Be patient. You may not have to spend money to have your pin be discovered. Sometimes, it's a matter of the content being of high value or interest at a particular point of time. Sometimes all it takes is for a major blogger with a big audience to re-pin you. Wait for the pin to get some traction before you start promoting it. Make sure it's a money maker before you throw money at it.

Tips to Ace Your Promoted Pin Campaigns

Alright, chief. Let's ace your promoted pin goals and amplify your Pinterest account and sales. I'll give you some pointers and best practices to get you moving in the right direction, and hopefully save you a ton of money and increase your sales at the same time.

Focus on creativity. Beautiful, helpful, and focused pins win the race for Pinterest ads. Be sure to add your branding on the bottom or lower corner for brand tagging. Your pin ad should be tall and have a few different images with text overlaying on top. Speak to your reader like it's a conversation. Ask a question. Use the word "you". These are creative ways to get your pin noticed and clicked on.

Test mode. It's going to take longer than a week to really gauge whether your pin campaign is working. A pin campaign might require a whole month to make any sort of firm conclusion. So be patient with this process if you're not seeing traffic right away. Give it some time! Go into test mode, just like I have in the past, to see how things work for you and commit yourself to learning how things work for *your* brand.

Don't run more than one pin advertisement per campaign. Pinterest will tell you which pin is performing the best. The best performing pin will be shown the most. The others will be dropped off eventually and you won't be able to see which pin design is working for you the best. You need to know specific results. So stick with one pin at a time.

Use 30-50 keywords in targeting your audience. Use keywords people actually search for in looking for a product like yours. "Crazy amazing template" is not a good search term. However, "Canva recipe template" is more long-tail and specific. So drop the adjectives and action words and stick to nouns and keyword descriptions only. You don't need to be repetitive, and if you go over the limit of keywords you won't be punished by Pinterest. I know some businesses and brands use around 200 keywords with zero negative impact.

Select all devices. In the beginning, you should choose "all" devices when promoting on Pinterest. It'll give you more reach and amplification. 80% of Pinners use Pinterest on an IOS mobile device, so keep that in the back of your head when you're advertising.

What is the difference between a daily budget and a lifetime budget? Obviously, a daily budget will cap at the end of each day. A lifetime budget actually works pretty much the same way; you just commit the entire budget up front and Pinterest breaks it down for you.

Limited targeting impacting your results? If your audience and keyword use target is limited, your results will also be limited. Sometimes over-niching impacts the creative aspect of your pin and audience, which limits your positive results. Expand and let those keywords and pin images expand a bit.

Install the Pinterest conversion tracker. Definitely take the time to do that install. Get the code put in. Getting all that valuable data leads to better choices and use of your time.

Look at your Engaged Click Through Rate. This is what tells you how well your pins are getting clicked through versus re-pinned. Click-throughs indicate interest and the triggered desire to learn more. This is often more important than anything else.

Check your ECTR and ECPC results. If your ECTR (Effective Click Through Rate) is rising and your ECPC (Earned Cost Per Click) is dropping then you're doing something right. I recommend checking this every 30 days when you're running Pinterest ads.

Turn your landing page ads off on promoted pin pages. When you're running ads, you want all the attention on your product or landing page. Therefore, when you're spending money, you don't want the pinner focused on anything else. So be sure to turn of any MediaVine, Google Adsense or ShareASale ads if you're running them on your site for those landing pages receiving paid traffic. Why pay for people to come on over only to have them leave and click on an advertisement? Don't let your reader get distracted!

How to Monetize Pinterest Traffic

Pinterest Stats

Most people find my blog through Pinterest. It accounts for 80% of my traffic. Second in line is YouTube, which is an area I've focused on more this year, and have received positive results from that, as well. Third in line is direct traffic, which increase this year when I launched a membership access program with unlimited access to my website's designs, products, courses, books, etc.

I watch my Pinterest stats pretty closely and monitor them daily. I watch what my audience is interested in, and if it's related to my core topics, I'll put more and more content out that my audience loves, using my content modifier method, and uploading in intervals to keep the traffic coming in nonstop.

Keep delivering the content your audience loves, and make it easy for them to follow you on the channel of their choice.

There are ways to make money from your Pinterest efforts if you get your site properly set up to make money from ads.

AD REVENUE FROM PINTEREST TRAFFIC

One of the things I noticed when I was bringing in traffic from Pinterest was that my Google Adsense RPM was increasing, bringing in more ad revenue when I was actively pinning more from my domain.

In this case, more pins = more traffic = more Google Adsense income.

I view Adsense as a bonus way to add income to your site. It pays for hosting, improvements, subscriptions like Tailwind, new images, etc. So just from the ad income money alone, you could run your entire blog and even pay for your time blogging and writing for it.

In my eyes, it's not a solid long-term strategy or big money maker. It pays for the little things and ongoing costs.

But for beginning bloggers and bloggers who are in the midst of testing things and conducting research, Google Adsense is a viable option. In fact, all the money you might spend on Pinterest promoted pins could be earned back and then some just through your Google Adsense income, based on your Adsense Page RPM. Page RPM is the average earnings per thousand page views. It's calculated based on a combination of your traffic, CTR (click-through-rate), and CPC (cost per click).

Page RPM = (Estimated earnings / Number of page views) * 1000

So if your page got 1000 views, and your page RPM is $3.46, you'd be page $3.46 for that day. Anywhere from $2-5 is considered on the low end. On the medium end, a good page RPM is $5-10. High end is anything above $10.

When you have custom traffic coming in, you'll tend to earn more. Let's say you have some high-value keywords on your post and three ads running on it. If the ad is seen and clicked on, then your page is earning money. There are different types of ads. Some ads while earn more money than others, just as the placement of some ads will make more income than others.

Don't fall for the trap that some bloggers state when they say that people aren't clicking on ads in a banner or sidebar, and that you have to insert everything in your post. That's actually untrue, as I've had a lot of sidebar activity and click-throughs on banners. You're not going to know if sidebar and banner ads work for your particular blog unless you try them.

And don't forget about brands—you may find some that will be willing to pay you big money if your posts are demonstrating high-traffic, high-engagement induced clicks off of ads. When working with brands, make sure you're shutting off other ads you might have running on those particular posts. Brands pay more for traffic you drive to them, so you want people clicking on the brand links, and nowhere else.

CPM (cost per mille) ads in your banner and sidebar along with your posts will also earn you money—a certain amount based on every 1,000 people who see them. The more Pinterest traffic you get, the more you're going to be page just on CPM ads. So even though you may not have clickable ads in your post, you could earn money from banners and sidebars, based on how CPM ads are paid out.

Final Tips on Ads

There are a few ad companies you can partner with without much hassle. Google Adsense is obviously the first choice bloggers go to, MediaVine is for bloggers with 75k unique sessions per month (as of the date of publication), and there is Sovereign. The ad code is easy to create and install, and you're allowed to set minimums so you're in more control than with Google Adsense or MediaVine.

Check to see if you're able to use Amazon ads. You'll be able to know if it's available on your dashboard. Their code is also easy to set up and the ads start displaying quickly.

Watch for slowness of page load. Some ad companies' codes will slow down your site. Drop them like a hot potato if you're noticing a slow page load speed.

Mobile ads. Google will penalize your site via the search engine if your site isn't mobile friendly. You *want* to have as on your mobile site. It's a great tap-worthy asset to have for mobile users who are curious and bored out of their minds standing or sitting around.

Put up your own ads. Pro blogger tip! If you really want to boost conversion of your own products, or if you're just getting started and haven't been approved with any ad companies yet, you can try creating in-post ads for your own materials. Using your own domain real estate, you can create beautiful images and link them to your products in your shop. For example, if you have a book published on Amazon, instead of sending them out to Amazon, you can link it to a page or a blog post on your site that talks about the book first, and *then* link it out to the Amazon product. Take steps to keep the reader on your site. This will also increase your CPM revenue, because the longer you keep the reader on your site, the more they will see your CPM ads.

Choose your keywords wisely. Choose keywords not to rank first on Google, but to help brands find you. Use the Google keyword planner, and you'll discover which keywords and long-tail keyword phrases are more valuable than others next to the keyword. Those bid amounts are what the companies and brands are willing to pay for those keywords. Keep in mind that the amounts listed there aren't a guarantee; whatever you make on the keyword is actually split with Google Adsense.

Finally, be sure to paste your metadata and keywords into the

Alt tag on Pinterest images. Those images will then have keywords that people will want to click on, and will increase your traffic on Pinterest.

Conclusion

I'm hoping you have enough information here to know when and why to promote pins for your content. Part of the process of amplifying your reach is to find people you normally wouldn't using your typical channels. You have your blog, your email subscribers, your tribes, and the traffic coming in from people who are searching or are interested in posts like yours. But you can promote on Pinterest to make that reach go even further.

Follow my advice—test your landing pages first and make sure you have conversions happening *before* you start throwing money at ads. I have found Pinterest ads to be extraordinarily helping in extending reach. I did *not* use them during my testing between December 2018 and February 2019 to grow my account. They have a time and place. I'd rather watch you grow organically first, see you get natural, organic traffic from Pinterest first and then succeed with Pinterest promoted ads after that.

Try giving promoted pins a try. I think you'll like the results, which will surpass any other ad you've created on social media platforms.

7 AWARENESS METHOD

THE LAST METHOD that we're going to cover is the awareness method. There are several ways to build awareness to your brand using Pinterest besides promoting your content with promoted pins.

We're going to cover 6 ways that you can use to amplify others' awareness of your Pinterest account and pins besides using a paid awareness approach with promoted pins.

- Social Media
- Post or Page Articles
- In-Post Ads—Widgets
- Pinterest-Specific Promotions
- Blog Icons & Buttons
- Email Marketing

So let's get to these various avenues of amplifying your Pinterest reach through all the resources you can tap into.

Social Media

I'm not big on social media, in that while I may have decent numbers and followers, I'm not a huge fan of it. While I think social media is filled with a lot of vanity, selfies, and posts needing likes and affirmation. But it's here to stay, in one form or another, and people are on various platforms for a reason.

But I do think that as you grow on Pinterest and challenge yourself to a race against your own self, that you'll find you require less and less affirmation on social media and will appreciate the disconnect from all the drama that seems to thrive on those kinds of networks.

One thing that Gary Vaynerchuk has said that stuck with me that relates a great deal to Pinterest is that when you're creating content on any kind of platform, you need to be in the mindset of what your reader or customer is into for that particular platform.

Instagram users love pretty images.

Facebook users love... drama? Statuses? Communicating directly with friends? Articles? It's really hard to know anymore with that one.

Twitter users love succinctness. You can only get so many

characters into a post so you have to be clever in getting a tweet out.

SnapChat users love their filters. (I don't even bother with this one.)

LinkedIn users are on the platform for more business-minded opportunities and networking.

Pinterest users want to be inspired and discover and learn new things.

YouTube users love watching videos and being entertained.

You get the point...

And Gary's absolutely *right*. You have to cater to the mindset of the user on the platform that they're on. I'm certainly not going to go on LinkedIn and post pictures of my kids' artwork. That seems more Instagram-ish.

YouTube. Yes, you can actually use YouTube to promote your Pinterest account. If you're making videos and embedding them on your website from your YouTube channel, and pushing traffic to your YouTube channel, why not push traffic from YouTube to Pinterest, too?

As you may have guessed, my focus areas have been search-based engines like Pinterest, Google, YouTube, Etsy, etc. YouTube became my next focus in 2019 and it became apparent to me that many of the search knowledge I developed by learning how to amplify on Pinterest applied to YouTube, as well. But I'm just getting started.

The one thing I did notice though was that when I was mentioning some of the things I was doing on Pinterest, my Pinterest account got flooded with more activity on the days I posted videos about Pinterest. There's no reason why you couldn't have traffic directed to Pinterest account-specific activities to grow your follower base, just like anything else.

In addition, with video, YouTube and Pinterest go hand in hand. Both are search-based, both have users looking for channels and accounts like yours who specialize in your unique topic. You could actually grow both.

I've noticed that YouTube does take quite a bit more time than Pinterest ever has, and for that reason, in 2019, I've done what I've been able to do from a time commitment perspective. Like Pinterest, you're going to want to gauge how much time you can or are willing to commit to marketing. I'd love to get to a point where I was as confident with YouTube as I am with Pinterest.

Learning and mastering skills one at a time takes just that… time.

So when you get an opportunity and feel like you have your Pinterest game on par (10 million in monthly views, keeping that traffic, and over 400k monthly page views on your blog), venture into YouTube and start grabbing an audience over there. You're going to find remarkable similarities to Pinterest that I think will help reduce the learning curve.

Facebook. One way to get followers from your friends list or your business Facebook page is to highlight other Pinterest accounts that are applicable to a specific audience you have on Facebook. For example, I know a lot of other authors on Facebook, and I've pinned a fair amount about writing as a career choice. And I have a few writing boards that are quite helpful for writers at all stages in their career (*it's one that requires a high degree of self discipline, by the way—not an easy career by any means*).

One of the articles I wrote was about other accounts and boards to follow if you're a writer. Of course, I recommended following one of my writing boards. The post was a smashing hit. I still get activity from it and I wrote it back in late 2017, if I recall. So that one article I shared with my friends and posted on my Facebook page got more Pinterest traffic and re-pins. Even though it was about Pinterest, it still garnered a lot of additional traffic I wouldn't have had, and I've been told it reignited a passion in some for Pinterest and finding great writing advice. That made me feel good, because I love Pinterest and there's a lot of solid information and tutorials on there.

I think Facebook is more of a plethora of different kinds of content, so you're safe in posting blog articles you've written on there, along with ideas and things you've discovered on Pinterest.

If you're going to use Facebook, I would recommend posting and sharing a landing page you've created that has an embed of your Pinterest profile in it, and encourages people to follow you on that platform.

Twitter. Twitter is a unique beast because you have to be short and to the point. I ran a lot of unscientific tests with Pinterest and Twitter, and got some interesting results. You have the ability to auto-tweet pins to your Twitter account from Pinterest and Tailwind, as well.

Include special Tweetable elements in your posts and pages specific to Twitter users like install Cick-to-Tweet quotes within your pages and posts. This allows your Twitter visitors to tweet the highlights onto their account. In addition, it can help spur some growth on your Twitter account, as well.

When attracting Twitter folks, encourage them to follow you on Pinterest too, and share the benefits of following you there. Highlight some ideas for them that a succinct Twitter user who might enjoy conversion and wit would love to know more about regarding your topic.

LinkedIn. LinkedIn is a business network of people looking for all kinds of opportunities—but mostly framed around doing business and making connections. What pins or articles do you have, related to your niche, that touch on the elements of business that you could share?

Maybe you have a board that features business-type articles and pins that your LinkedIn network might enjoy. Be sure to create a few landing pages specifically for your LinkedIn crowd, too. These are generally people looking to network and see who's talented at doing whatever you might be making a career out of.

Instagram. Show off those pretty pins, just in square form! You can easily resize things in Canva with a Pro account. You could even show pictures of yourself prepping your pins for release or designing them. Sharing your workspace is also pretty popular, as are authentic photos of you working. Explain what you're doing and why you love blogging. Let your followers in on your process and why you feel joy doing what you do. They'll love it…

WHATEVER YOU CHOOSE to do to use the audience you already have is up to you. I've had people transfer over and follow me on Pinterest just to see what I'm up to based on ideas I've posted or pins I've shared that are new and unique to them. It's just something I think you should try, at least. You don't have to give up on social media altogether, but maybe just dedicate more of your time elsewhere more productive instead of committing yourself to replying back and forth on comments and feeds.

Hint—Pinterest is drama free. You'll love it. It's freeing.

Post or Page Articles

Another way to bring more awareness to your Pinterest account and feed is to put leaderboard images regarding specials you might have specifically for your Pinterest crowd or where they can get more ideas related to your page or post's topic. A basic image with the Pinterest icon in red along with a "Follow me on Pinterest to see ALL the great ideas about

____ here"—and then make the image clickable and linked out to your Pinterest profile.

Some have decided to use a plugin called MiloTree, which costs money every month. You don't need it. You're not *going* to need it if you follow these methods. Plus, those sidebar popups that stick to the side of the screen have all sorts of outbound branding for the company that could detract people away from your site. Plus, in my opinion, as a designer, they're clunky looking and I know you want your website looking sharp, so don't use it. You don't need it, and it's just an extra added cost.

In-Post Ads—Widgets

Pinterest has a widget builder that is perfect for sidebar and in-post or page additions.

You can start building your widgets here:

https://business.pinterest.com/en/pinterest-widget-builder

From save button, follow button, pin widget, profile widget to board widget, you have a lot of options to create embeds within your content to encourage people to follow a board or your profile, save your content to Pinterest, or even see what else you might have to offer on a specific board.

Get them clicking!

Pinterest-Specific Promotions

Some Pinterest business users have chosen to make certain specials exclusive to their Pinterest audience. I have done this. It's is super cool. This could be a discount that only Pinterest users see, and leads them to a Pinterest audience only landing page. I've even seen some pages where you can log in using your Pinterest account to access landing pages, which would be a great challenge for you to implement if you're able to get that techie.

There's a higher disposable income on Pinterest anyway, than any other form of social media offers, so why not let them shop and encourage them to special offers?

Blog Icons & Buttons

Dont' forget your blog icons and buttons. These are no-brainers but I see so many blogs and websites missing their Pinterest link buttons everywhere. If Pinterest is where you want to focus and drive your audience, then maybe only have your Pinterest icon and email icon available. It lets people know 'hey, I'm dedicated to this platform'. They can always discover you on other channels. But if your *best* content is on Pinterest, by all means, lead them there.

Email Marketing

I still share pins, recipes, ideas, and articles via pin images with my email list, depending on which list is applicable for that kind of content. If they found me on Pinterest, I'm going to keep that whole look and feel alive with Pinterest-type images and content.

Let your audience know you're collecting all sorts of pins and ideas related to a specific challenge you're trying to solve. Share other bloggers' pins and show your confidence and security about being a blogger willing to share a slice of the attention pie. Highlight other bloggers regularly so you can show your audience you're committed to helping them and introducing other people to help, as well.

Be cool like that. It looks good on you.

All of these areas lead to more awareness of your Pinterest activity and profile, which leads your audience right back to your website. Activity on your website helps build trust, relationships, and gives value. Your wisdom means a great deal to your audience. So nudge them over there and help them solve their challenges that you already know how to overcome. *I know you have a lot of hidden talent you're probably not tapping into; this is your time!*

Conclusion

Let people know you're active on Pinterest and where to get education, additional tutorials, and knowledge. Let them know some of your *best* work is on there. That will help make sure that your existing followers see even more of you.

Write articles that support your Pinterest activities but also cater to the audience you're attracting, based on the medium you use for social media. Don't forget to advertise yourself with your own ads in your posts and pages. And show off your boards and Pinterest profile using the widgets available!

Then, put your blog icons and buttons to use to encourage plenty of clicking and following behavior. Don't ignore your existing email marketing list of followers who already love your content. Be sure to draw them back into your world with Pinterest-specific love that they can share with their followers.

It's time to put it all together! This has been fun, and I've enjoyed teaching you these methods, and I hope you had fun, too. Check out some of the other books available to you to really get ahead and challenge yourself as a blogger and writer.

Looking forward to seeing your results soon!

AFTERWORD

Pinterest nerds forever! Thanks for reading!

ABOUT THE AUTHOR

Kerrie Legend is a professional blogger and writer at kerrielegend.com. She is a blogger's blogger, excitedly creating templates and designs for bloggers to save time and money in creating content upgrades for their own readers. She is happily married and raises six boys in Montana. When she's not fly fishing, she's writing, designing, and teaching online courses.

A huge advocate of Pinterest marketing, Kerrie has focused intensely in helping entrepreneurs build their brands, email lists, and followers on one of the largest search engines on the planet. In 2019, she grew her account from 80k monthly viewers to over 14+ million through her own research.

She enjoys making charcuterie boards, homeschooling her boys, bullet journaling, acquiring copious amounts of notebooks, has a passion for stone paper, buys ink by the barrel, and slings 10,000-15,000 words on paper a day.

 pinterest.com/kerrielegend

ALSO BY KERRIE LEGEND

100 Pinterest Marketing Business Tips

Email Marketing Magic: Lead Magnets, Sales Funnels, Opt-in Freebies, and Content Upgrades - from Amateur to Expert

Pinterest Marketing: 80k to 14+ Million in 3 Months

Art of Blogging: Website Traffic, Writing Copy, and Email Marketing

Copy Cocktail: How to Write Yummy Word that Convert & Delight

How to Make Money with Your Writing

50 Ways to Improve Your Website

100 Ways to Re-Purpose Your Content

Made in the USA
Middletown, DE
30 November 2020